BEGINNER'S GUIDE TO SELLII
ON ETS

How To Start Your Own Home-Based Business with Printable Products

BY ANN ECKHART

BEGINNER'S GUIDE TO SELLING DIGITAL PRODUCTS ON ETSY

INTRODUCTION

CHAPTER ONE: TYPES OF DIGITAL PRODUCTS

CHAPTER TWO: WHAT YOU NEED TO CREATE DIGITAL PRODUCTS

CHAPTER THREE: CREATING DIGITAL PRODUCTS

CHAPTER FOUR: OPENING AN ETSY SHOP

CHAPTER FIVE: LISTING DIGITAL PRODUCTS ON ETSY

CHAPTER SIX: MANAGING YOUR ETSY SHOP

CHAPTER SEVEN: HANDLING CUSTOMER SERVICE ISSUES

CHAPTER EIGHT: ADVERTISING & MARKETING YOUR PRODUCTS

CHAPTER NINE: ETSY ACCOUNTING MADE EASY

CHAPTER TEN: HOW TO GROW YOUR DIGITAL PRODUCT BUSINESS

CONCLUSION

ABOUT THE AUTHOR

COPYRIGHT 2023 ANN ECKHART

COVER DESIGN BY ANN ECKHART

INTRODUCTION

I started my first home-based company in 2005, and over the years I've created multiple e-commerce businesses. I've sold wholesale, liquidation, and second-hand thrifted goods on eBay, Amazon, Etsy, and Poshmark. I have built a successful author business through Amazon KDP writing books such as the one you are reading right now. I run two YouTube channels. I started an Etsy sticker shop. And I've created affiliate marketing income streams from blogging and social media.

While all of the businesses I have run have pros and cons, there is one that stands out as being the easiest to start, and that is selling digital products on Etsy.

Digital products, which are also known as digital downloads or printables, offer sellers the ability to sell downloadable files without having to worry about sourcing, storing, or shipping inventory. Since the product is digital, there's no need to update files once they're uploaded, and customer service is minimal. When a customer purchases a digital product, they receive the file, download it to their computer, and print it themselves, making the process simple and hassle-free for both the buyer and seller.

So how does this whole thing work? To sell a digital download online, a seller creates a PDF file of their product and lists it for sale on various platforms. On Etsy specifically, when a customer purchases the download, Etsy provides them with instructions on how to download the file to their system. Etsy then automatically deducts its fees and deposits the profits into the seller's account. Unless the product requires the seller to customize it, there is no communication between the buyer and seller.

Digital downloads are true list-it-and-forget-it products. Unlike print-on-demand products where a seller needs to be on top of orders and customer service issues, digital downloads require little work on the part of sellers. You as a seller list a digital download once and then collect the profits for as long as the item remains for sale.

Etsy, in particular, is the top-selling site for these types of digital products. And while I will cover selling printables on all of the major websites, selling on Etsy will be the main focus of this book as it is truly the best place to start a digital product business.

Etsy is an e-commerce website that's known as a place for artists and crafters to sell their wares. However, Etsy also provides a platform for people to sell vintage items such as antiques and collectibles. Additionally, there's a growing print-on-demand business model on Etsy, where sellers can connect their accounts with third-party print providers and offer a range of products, from t-shirts to coffee mugs, printed with their own designs.

However, making crafts, sourcing vintage items, and designing tee shirts not only require a lot of time but also an upfront investment and a continual flow of cash to keep finding new items to sell. On the other hand, digital products offer a unique business opportunity that almost anyone can start without spending much money.

So, why is Etsy such a great website for digital downloads? After all, PDF files aren't exactly crafts or antiques. They aren't even tangible products but rather files.

Unlike other major e-commerce platforms such as Amazon, eBay, Poshmark, and Mercari, Etsy allows sellers to list and sell downloadable files in a variety of formats. While Amazon permits sellers to upload eBook files for Kindle devices, they don't allow for the sale of downloadable PDF files. Likewise, eBay used to permit digital file listings, but they no longer do. Neither Poshmark nor Mercari allows digital downloads, either. This means that Etsy is the only major e-commerce platform that enables people to sell digital downloads.

And while other websites allow the sale of digital downloads, such as Redbubble and Gumroad, the traffic and sales numbers of these platforms pale in comparison to Etsy. Etsy boosts nearly 80 million active buyers, which is a massive audience for sellers to tap into.

And as Etsy continues to invest in its business, the buyer pool continues to grow.

When it comes to digital downloads specifically, Etsy has become a significant player in the market with total marketplace sales for digital downloads at nearly $350 million, which represents a substantial increase compared to the previous year. Etsy's massive traffic and sales numbers make it the best platform for digital creators.

In addition to high traffic and sale numbers, Etsy's fee structure and ease of listing also make it great for even beginners to list and sell printables. Etsy charges a listing fee of $0.20 per item for a four-month listing period, and they also charge a transaction fee of 5% on the total sale price, which includes shipping costs. This fee structure is competitive with other e-commerce platforms and allows sellers to keep more of their profits. As an example, eBay charges around 35 cents to list an item just for one month and also takes a higher percentage of the final sale price.

Furthermore, Etsy makes it simple for sellers to list their printable products for sale. Sellers can upload their files, add a title and description, and set a price in a matter of minutes. Once the listing is live, it's visible to millions of potential buyers who are on the site daily. This makes it easy for sellers to get their products in front of a large audience and start making sales quickly. And sellers don't have to worry about keeping inventory to sell; all of their items are digital files that are stored online.

So, what type of person would make a good Etsy digital product shop owner? Many assume you need to have extensive graphic design experience or be a computer expert. However, you don't need to be a graphic designer or IT professional to start and grow a successful digital product business. In fact, creating and selling digital downloads on Etsy is a relatively easy process that almost anyone can learn. While having design skills or technical knowledge can certainly be helpful, it's not a requirement for starting an Etsy shop.

One of the great things about selling digital products on Etsy is that there is a wide range of complexity when it comes to the various digital products. Some digital products may require advanced design skills, such as intricate illustrations or complex vector graphics, while others may be as simple as creating a one-page PDF document. And in many cases you do not even have to design your own files; you can purchase ready-to-sell files from other designers.

In this book, I will walk you step-by-step through the entire process of researching, creating, and listing digital products for sale on Etsy. We'll go over the following:

- The types of digital products you can sell

- Understanding the various categories and niches of digital products
- What equipment and skills are necessary for creating digital products
- Where to purchase ready-made digital files to sell
- How to create various digital products
- How to set up your Etsy shop
- How to list digital products on Etsy
- How to effectively manage your Etsy shop
- How to handle customer service issues
- How to promote your Etsy shop
- Etsy accounting made easy
- How to grow your digital business beyond Etsy

If you are willing to put in the work and follow the steps laid out in this book, you'll be on your way to opening your very own Etsy shop selling digital products and earning passive income from home. And once you've mastered selling these products on Etsy, you can expand to other e-commerce platforms to earn even more money!

Selling digital downloads can be a side hustle to earn some extra income or a full-time business from which you support your family. How big you want to grow this business and how much money you want to make is completely up to you!

CHAPTER ONE: TYPES OF DIGITAL PRODUCTS

Before diving into the process of creating digital products to sell online, it's important to first understand the various types of digital products you can create. Digital products are a broad category that covers a wide range of items, from art prints to templates, worksheets, and more. This diversity is one of the strengths of the digital product market, as it means that you can find a product category that you enjoy and that suits your skill level.

When choosing the type of digital product you want to create, it's important to consider your interests. If you love to draw illustrations, you might consider creating printable art or designs for digital scrapbooking. If you have a talent for writing, you might consider creating guided journal pages or digital planners. If you enjoy marketing, you might consider creating templates for social media or branding.

With digital products, there is something for everyone. By narrowing down to focus on what you are already knowledgeable about, you'll have an easier time figuring out what products to create. It's important to choose a type of digital product that you will have fun creating and selling over the long term. If you don't like what you're doing, you're going to grow tired of it quickly, and creating digital products can become tedious after a while. That's why it's essential to choose a type of product that you're passionate about and that you're excited to work on each day. When you're creating something you love, it shows in the quality of your work, and customers will respond by ordering from you.

There are **several main categories of digital products**, and all have specific niches under them. When it comes to selling digital products under one store, such as within an Etsy shop, you want to focus on ONE category. This will help you build a brand that you can grow. For example, if you offer wedding invitations and business resumes in the same shop, customers may be confused. But if you start with wedding invitations, you can grow your shop to eventually include other types of digital wedding products and become a shop that brides can turn to for all of their wedding printables.

Size: Before we cover the various categories of digital products, it's important to note that the vast majority of digital downloads are 8.5" by 11", which is Letter Size. This is the standard print size for home printers, which is what the majority of customers will be using to print their digital purchases. Certain products, such as logos or other graphic design elements, are not printed out. For example, digital logos that customers will then insert into their social media platforms. But most of the products we'll be discussing in this book are printable.

While some sellers offer different sizes of products, they are targeting buyers who have different printer capabilities. For example, some shops offer digital sticker sheets that require the customer to be able to print different sizes of sticker paper but also have a cutting machine to cut the stickers out. Since this is a beginner's guide book we'll be focusing on standard 8.5" by 11" downloads. I will note if this is not the standard size in the categories where it applies.

Creating Products: We'll be covering the process of creating these products in Chapter Three of this book. This chapter is focused on the types of products themselves and helps you narrow down your category and niche. To get a visual idea of exactly what these products look like, simply do an Etsy search to see what other sellers are offering, and then think about how you can make something different that still fits into the same niche.

ORGANIZATION: The organization category for digital downloads encompasses a wide variety of niches, including:

Appointment Trackers: Appointment trackers help individuals keep track of their appointments, meetings, and events. Appointment trackers often include sections for the date, time, location, and purpose of the appointment. Some appointment trackers may also include space for additional notes, reminders, or follow-up actions.

Appointment trackers can be customized and tailored to meet the unique needs of the user. Some may include pre-filled dates and times, while others may be left blank for the user to fill in themselves. Offering a variety of the same page with different options such as some with pre-filled dates and some without is a great way to reach more customers. You can also tailor these appointment sheets to various individuals based on their occupations or household makeup.

Budget Trackers: Budget trackers help individuals manage their finances by keeping track of their income and expenses. Budget trackers typically include categories for income, expenses, and savings. Users can fill in their expected income and expenses for the month, and then track their actual income and expenses as they occur. Some budget trackers may also include sections for debt payments, savings goals, or investment tracking.

Budget trackers can be used by anyone from students and professionals to families and retirees. You can easily create one basic design for a budget page and then make some small edits to customize it for different customers. For example, a budget tracker used by a single person with no children would be different from a budget tracker used by a family of twelve.

Calendars: Calendars help individuals keep track of dates, events, and appointments throughout the year. Calendars typically include all 12 months of the year, with each month displayed on a separate page. They may include a variety of formats, such as a traditional grid format, a list format, or a planner-style format. Some calendars may also include additional sections for notes, goals, or reminders.

Calendars are used by people of all ages and from all walks of life. Offering a wide range of different calendars, both set designs and ones that can per personalized by the user, will help you attract more customers than simply offering one type of page. Since most calendars are dated, you'll need to update your products every year to reflect the new dates. Users hang these printouts on their refrigerators using magnets or put them into binders.

Cleaning Checklists: Cleaning checklists help individuals keep track of household cleaning tasks and chores. Cleaning checklists typically include a list of cleaning tasks that need to be completed, such as dusting, vacuuming, and scrubbing. They may be broken down by room, or by task type, and can also include a frequency guide, such as daily, weekly, or monthly tasks.

These digital products are for individuals who want to maintain a clean and organized living space but struggle with keeping track of all the necessary tasks. They can be used by anyone from students and professionals to families and retirees. By creating different checklists for different living situations, you'll maximize your customer base. Some customers like complex cleaning checklists while others like simple ones. Search Etsy to see what the current best-selling checklists are and then figure out how you can create something different to target a customer that isn't currently being served.

Daily Routines Schedules: Daily routine schedules help individuals plan and organize their daily activities and tasks. Daily routine schedules typically include a list of activities or tasks to be completed at specific times throughout the day. They may include sections for morning routines, work or school schedules, and evening routines. They are often in checklist style so that users can check each task as they complete it.

Some daily routine schedules may also include additional sections for self-care, exercise, or hobbies. Sellers who create these types of printable sheets have a wide variety available for different ages, locations, and stations in life. For example, the daily routine of a college student is much different than that of a retiree. How can you create unique schedules that target all of the different customers that are shopping for them?

Daily/Weekly/Monthly Planners: Planner downloads help individuals plan and organize their schedules and activities. Instead of a pre-bound book planner, printable planner pages are often put into binders by the customer. Since many people like daily planners but find the bound book versions too thick to manage, utilizing digital downloads makes setting up one's planner much easier.

Daily planners typically include a section for each day of the week, with space for scheduling appointments, tasks, and other activities. They may also include additional sections for notes, to-do lists, and goal setting.

Weekly planners typically include a section for each week of the year, with space for scheduling appointments, tasks, and other activities for each day of the week. They may also include sections for goal setting, habit tracking, and meal preparation.

Monthly planners typically include a section for each month of the year, with space for scheduling appointments, tasks, and other activities for each day of the month. They may also include budgeting pages and space to write down birthdays, anniversaries, and other special occasions.

Decluttering Checklists: Decluttering checklists help individuals simplify and organize their living space by breaking down the decluttering process into manageable tasks. Decluttering checklists typically include a list of tasks or areas of focus to be completed as part of the decluttering process. These tasks may include purging unnecessary items, organizing storage spaces, and deep cleaning.

Some decluttering checklists may also include tips and strategies for staying motivated and focused throughout the process. Think of how different people have different decluttering needs and develop printables for different living situations.

Family Organization Tools: Family organization printables can include a variety of different products, including:

- **Chore charts** help organize household tasks and assign them to family members.
- **Family calendars** help keep track of important dates and appointments for all family members.
- **Meal planners** help plan meals in advance and ensure that the family is eating healthily.
- Shopping lists to help organize weekly grocery shopping and ensure that nothing is forgotten.
- **Babysitter information sheets** provide necessary information to babysitters, such as emergency contacts, schedules, and routines.
- **Emergency contact lists** ensure that all important phone numbers and addresses are easily accessible in case of an emergency.
- **Family budget trackers** help manage family finances and ensure that bills are paid on time.
- **School information sheets** provide important information about school schedules, events, and contact information for teachers and staff.

- **Travel planners** help organize family vacations and keep track of reservations, flights, and activities.

Fitness Trackers: Fitness trackers help individuals track their fitness goals, progress, and routines. Fitness trackers typically include sections for tracking physical activity, such as steps taken, distance walked, or calories burned. They may also include sections for tracking exercise routines, such as weightlifting, running, or yoga. Some fitness trackers may also include sections for tracking nutrition, water intake, and sleep.

These digital products are for individuals who want to stay motivated and committed to their fitness goals, as they can provide a visual representation of progress and encourage accountability. They can be used by anyone from beginners to experienced athletes. Creating products for people wherever they are in their fitness journey ensures you maximize your potential customer base.

Goal Trackers: Goal trackers help individuals track and achieve their specific goals. Goal trackers typically include sections for setting specific, measurable, achievable, relevant, and time-bound (SMART) goals. Users can fill in their goals and track their progress over time, often through visual representations such as charts, graphs, or checklists.

Some goal trackers may also include sections for identifying potential obstacles, developing strategies to overcome them, and celebrating successes. These digital products are for individuals who want to stay focused and motivated in achieving their goals, whether they are related to personal development, career advancement, or other areas of interest. They can be used by anyone from students and professionals to retirees and hobbyists. Creating goal trackers specifically for every age and interest will help you maximize your potential sales.

Habit Trackers: Habit trackers help individuals track their daily or weekly habits and develop new routines. These digital products usually come in the form of printable templates that can be downloaded and printed from the convenience of one's home. They can be used in place of or in conjunction with goal trackers

Habit trackers typically include a list of habits that the user wants to develop or habits the user wants to break. Space is included for tracking progress over time. Users can fill in the habits they want to track and mark them off as they are completed each day or week. Some habit trackers may also include sections for identifying potential obstacles to habit formation, developing strategies to overcome them, and celebrating successes.

These digital products are for individuals who want to develop new habits, such as exercising regularly, eating healthily, or practicing self-care. Or they can be used to break habits such as drinking, smoking, or eating junk food.

Home Management Binders: Home management binders are digital download packs that help individuals organize and manage their important household information and tasks. They are referred to as "binders" because they contain numerous pages that the customer will put into a binder. However, you can also sell these sheets individually to maximize your sales potential as some customers may only want one or two of these pages. Digital products in this niche include:

- **Home inventory checklists** to keep track of household belongings and their value for insurance purposes.
- **Home maintenance schedules** to help organize routine home maintenance tasks such as HVAC maintenance or gutter cleaning.
- **Emergency preparedness checklists** ensure that the household is prepared for emergencies with necessary supplies, plans, and contacts.
- **Cleaning schedules** to help organize household cleaning tasks and ensure that each task is completed regularly.
- **Bill payment trackers** to keep track of bills and ensure that they are paid on time.
- **Meal planners and grocery lists** to plan meals in advance and ensure that the household is eating healthily.
- **Important contacts lists** to keep track of important contacts such as doctors, schools, and utility companies.

- **Home improvement project trackers** to help organize and keep track of home improvement projects.

Journal Inserts: Journal inserts provide additional pages or templates for users to add to their journals or planners. People who "Junk Journal" like to put their journals together using printables along with crafting techniques. Other people like to create their unique journal binders using a variety of different pages that are suited to their individual needs. Note that this is one niche where offering different sizes is beneficial most journals are smaller than 8.5" by 11".

Journal inserts can include a variety of templates, such as:

- **Gratitude journal pages** to help users practice daily gratitude and reflection.
- **Daily or weekly planner pages** help users plan their days and keep track of tasks and appointments.
- **Habit trackers** to help users track and develop new habits.
- **Mood trackers** help users track their emotional state over time.
- **Goal-setting templates** to help users set and achieve personal and professional goals.
- **Reflection and journaling prompts** inspire users to reflect on their thoughts and experiences.

Meal Planners: Meal planners help individuals plan and organize their meals in advance. Meal planners typically include sections for planning meals for breakfast, lunch, dinner, and snacks for a specific period, such as a week or a month. They may also include space for creating a grocery list, tracking food preferences or dietary restrictions, and recording meal prep or cooking notes.

These digital products are for individuals who want to maintain a healthy and balanced diet, save money on groceries, reduce food waste, or plan family meals more effectively. They can be used by anyone from busy professionals to families and retirees. Meal planners can be customized and tailored to meet the unique needs of the user. Some may include pre-filled meal categories, while others may be left blank for the user to fill in themselves. Consider all of the different diets and meal types that people eat to provide meal planners for as many potential customers as possible.

Password Trackers: Password trackers help individuals keep track of their online account usernames and passwords. Password trackers typically include sections for listing online account names, usernames, and passwords. They may also include sections for noting which email address is associated with each account, as well as any security questions and answers. These digital products are useful for individuals who have multiple online accounts and struggle to remember their login information. While most password trackers are pretty basic in their layout, you can create multiple varieties using different color patterns, fonts, quotes, and graphics.

Planner Pages: Planner pages provide additional sheets or templates for users to add to their planners or to use in place of the typical bound planner. Planner pages are different from daily/weekly/monthly planners in that they provide specific templates or pages for users to add to their existing planners or to use alone without a full planner. Ideas for these types of pages include goal setting, budget tracking, habit tracking, to-do lists, and even blank lined pages for note taking and journaling.

Daily/weekly/monthly planners typically include pre-dated pages for specific time periods, whereas planner pages provide more customizable options for users to add to their planners. Planner pages can be customized and tailored to meet the unique needs of the user. They can be designed with different themes, colors, and styles to match the user's preferences or branding, and can be printed in a variety of sizes and formats to match other planner products in a seller's shop.

Project Planners: Project planners help individuals plan and manage projects at both home and at work. Project planners typically include sections for identifying project goals, developing timelines and milestones, outlining tasks and responsibilities, and tracking progress over time. They may also include space for budgeting, resource allocation, risk assessment, and stakeholder communication. These digital products are for individuals who work on projects in various industries, such as business, education, healthcare, or personal development. Think of all the different industries that could use these types of downloads and tailor your designs to consider each.

Time Management Tools: Time management tools help people manage their time effectively, and efficiently, reduce stress, and improve productivity. They can be used by anyone from students and professionals to entrepreneurs and retirees, which gives you a great opportunity to create multiple products for a wide range of customers.

Time management tools can include a variety of digital products such as:

- **Time-blocking templates** to help users schedule their days and ensure that tasks are completed efficiently.
- **Prioritization worksheets** help users prioritize tasks and focus on the most important ones.
- **Time trackers** to help users track how they spend their time and identify areas where they can improve.
- **Distraction trackers** help users identify distractions and develop strategies to minimize them.

- **Pomodoro technique templates** help users work in focused intervals and take breaks in between.
- **Meeting agendas and note templates** to help users prepare for and document meetings efficiently.

To-Do Lists: To-do lists help individuals keep track of tasks they need to complete. To-do lists are practical and helpful tools for keeping track of tasks and ensuring that important tasks are not forgotten or overlooked. They can help users maintain focus, motivation, and accountability toward their goals and responsibilities.

To-do lists typically include sections for listing tasks that need to be completed, with checkboxes or other indicators for marking off tasks as they are completed. They may also include space for prioritizing tasks, setting deadlines, and adding notes or details about each task. While to-do list layouts are fairly redundant, you can set yours apart by using different colors, fonts, quotes, and graphics.

BUSINESS: Another large category for digital downloads is business. Product niches under this category include:

Resume Templates: Resume templates provide users with pre-designed page layouts for creating professional job resumes. These templates typically include a variety of sections, such as personal information, professional summary, work experience, education, skills, and references. They may also include space for adding a profile picture or other relevant images, such as logos or icons.

Some templates may also include industry-specific layouts or sections to highlight relevant skills or achievements. They provide an affordable alternative to hiring a professional resume writer and can be easily customized and updated as needed. By providing numerous templates for various industries, you will attract a much larger customer base than only designing basic templates.

Business Plan Templates: Business plan templates provide users with a pre-designed outline and format for creating a comprehensive business plan. Business plan templates typically include a variety of sections, such as an executive summary, company description, market analysis, competitive analysis, marketing and sales strategy, operations plan, and financial projections. They may also include space for adding charts, tables, and other relevant data to support the plan.

These digital products are for entrepreneurs and small business owners who need to develop a business plan to guide their operations and attract investors or lenders. Most banks require a business plan before lending money to new businesses. A well-crafted business plan can help entrepreneurs identify opportunities and challenges, clarify their business vision, and set achievable goals and strategies.

Invoice Templates: Invoice templates provide users with pre-designed layouts for creating professional invoices for their businesses. Invoice templates typically include a variety of sections, such as the business name and logo, customer information, invoice number, date, and payment terms. They may also include space for listing products or services provided, the quantity available, the price for each item, and the total amount due. Some templates may also include fields for tax calculations, discounts, or shipping and handling charges.

These digital products are for small business owners who need to create and send professional invoices to clients or customers. A well-crafted invoice can help businesses manage their finances, track payments, and ensure timely payments from clients or customers. Most invoice templates tend to be rather basic, but you can separate yours from the competition by offering a variety of color and font choices along with the option to add company logos to the forms.

Social Media Templates: Social media templates are different from printables in that they are designed to be used specifically for creating digital content for social media platforms, rather than being printed and used physically. This is one of the niches where the standard 8.5" by 11" Letter size of paper does not apply.

Social media templates are typically designed in specific sizes and dimensions that are optimized for different social media platforms, such as Instagram, Facebook, Twitter, YouTube, TikTok, and Pinterest. They are usually created as digital files that can be downloaded and edited on a computer or mobile device and then uploaded to social media platforms directly.

For example, some sellers sell custom banners for YouTube channels. The customer would order this service on Etsy, and then provide the seller with their logo and colors. The seller would then design the banner to fit the YouTube banner section. The seller would provide a digital copy of the banner to the customer. The customer would download the file and upload it directly to their YouTube channel.

Starting a social media template business means you will need to be a highly skilled graphic designer. You will also need to customize every product and it's common to give the client several options to choose from, along with allowing them to make one to two revisions. Customers may have a logo they want you to design banners and posts around, or they may be seeking out logo creation.

Marketing Materials: Marketing materials are pre-designed templates or files that businesses and individuals can use to create advertisements, such as flyers, brochures, business cards, and other promotional materials. These digital products can be downloaded and edited on a computer or mobile device, and then printed or shared online.

Marketing materials templates typically include a variety of designs, layouts, and styles that can be customized and tailored to meet the specific needs of the user. They may also include pre-written text and graphics that can be edited and adjusted to match the user's brand or message. These digital products are for small businesses, entrepreneurs, and marketers who want to create professional and cost-effective marketing materials quickly and easily. By using pre-designed templates, users can save time and effort in the design process and ensure that their materials have a consistent and professional look.

As with social media templates, sellers of marketing materials may need more advanced graphic design skills. You will not only need to design the layout of the materials themselves but also match colors to the logo provided by the client. It's common for sellers to create several options for their customers and to allow the customer to make one or two edits.

Business Finance Tracking Templates: Business finance tracking templates provide users with pre-designed pages for tracking and managing their income and expenses. Business finance tracking templates can include a variety of layouts, such as profit and loss statements, cash flow projections, balance sheets, and budget trackers. They also include space for tracking expenses, income, and taxes, as well as analyzing financial data to help the business make informed financial decisions.

By using pre-designed templates, businesses can save time in the financial tracking process and ensure that their financial records are accurate and up to date, which is especially important when it comes time to file taxes. Business finance tracking templates can be customized and tailored to meet the unique needs of the user. They can be designed with different themes, colors, and styles to match the user's preferences or branding. Some templates may also include industry-specific layouts or sections to address the unique financial aspects of a particular industry.

CRAFTING: The next category for digital products is crafting. Digital crafting products are one of the biggest categories of templates sold on Etsy. If you are a crafter yourself, you can narrow in on your field of expertise to create printable products for customers. However, you don't have to craft or even be a graphic designer to create some of these products.

Crochet Patterns: Crochet patterns are a niche in the crafting category that involves creating and selling digital patterns for crocheting various items, such as hats, scarves, blankets, and toys.

Crochet pattern digital downloads can include a variety of patterns, such as beginner-friendly patterns, advanced patterns, seasonal patterns, and themed patterns. They may also include detailed instructions, images, and diagrams to guide users through the crocheting process.

By using digital downloads, users can access a wide range of patterns quickly and easily, building up a library of patterns faster and cheaper than buying physical pattern books. Some patterns may also include variations or customization options to allow users to create unique and personalized items. Customers are typically drawn to shops that have an overall cohesive look, so sticking to one niche, say vintage-inspired patterns or patterns for Christmas, will help build your brand.

By offering a wide range of patterns for different abilities, you will attract a larger customer base. For example, perhaps you create a pattern for crocheting a baby blanket. However, rather than offering just one pattern, you create three, one for beginners, one for intermediate users, and one for highly skilled crocheters.

Quilting Patterns: Quilting pattern digital downloads are pre-designed templates that provide users with a variety of patterns for creating quilts. Quilting patterns can include a variety of templates, such as traditional quilt patterns, modern quilt patterns, baby quilt patterns, and seasonal quilt patterns. They may also include detailed instructions, images, and diagrams to guide users through the quilting process.

The same strategies for selling quilting patterns mimic those of selling crochet patterns.

Sewing Patterns: Sewing pattern digital downloads are pre-designed templates that provide users with a variety of patterns for creating clothes, bags, accessories, and other sewing projects. Sewing patterns can include a variety of templates, such as dress patterns, skirt patterns, bag patterns, and accessory patterns. They may also include detailed instructions, images, and diagrams to guide users through the sewing process.

The same strategies for selling sewing patterns mimic those of selling crochet and quilting patterns.

Coloring Book Pages: Coloring isn't just for kids anymore. Adult coloring books have become just as popular as those for children. Coloring book pages as digital downloads are pre-designed templates that users can print out and color. They can also print out the pages as many times as they want to color using different techniques and coloring tools.

Coloring book pages for adults especially are marketed as a way to relax. Coloring book pages can include a variety of designs, with mandalas, animals, flowers, and abstract patterns being the most popular. Sarcastic funny quotes, adult humor, and inspirational sayings are also popular trends in the coloring niche.

When selling coloring books as a set, you want the pattens to follow the same theme and target the same audience. For instance, you don't want one page to be a Halloween children's coloring page while the next is a complex mandala pattern geared towards grownups. Sellers can offer single pages or sets of pages, although single-page downloads are typically very complex designs. Otherwise, most sellers offer pages as a set or "book."

Wrapping Paper Patterns: If you are a graphic designer or artist, you can offer your artwork as wrapping paper patterns that users can download and print out themselves. Because most customers will only have access to a standard printer, they are often looking to wrap small gifts that will require only a sheet or two of paper. Although some commercial users may use a downloaded pattern to then create large sheets of wrapping.

Wrapping paper patterns can include a variety of templates, such as birthday wrapping paper, holiday wrapping paper, and patterned wrapping paper. They also include multiple designs and color variations to allow users to choose their preferred design. Offering customers the ability to personalize the design – such as adding names or dates – offers you the ability to charge more for wrapping paper downloads.

Stickers: Did you know that people can create their stickers using printers and cutting machines? Selling sticker digital downloads requires you to create sticker designs that the customer then downloads and prints out themselves. There's no need for you to invest in printers, cutters, and sticker paper; and there is no inventory for you to store.

Stickers can include a variety of themes such as decorative stickers, planner stickers, vinyl stickers for water bottles and laptops, and even wall decals. Some stickers may also include customization options to allow users to create unique and personalized stickers. For example, parents love to order stickers of their children's names. Once the digital sticker template is downloaded, the customer can print the stickers onto sticker paper or other printable adhesive materials using their printer. They can then cut out the stickers using scissors, a craft knife, or a cutting machine, such as a Cricut.

If you plan to sell planner pages, sticker sheets would make a nice addition to your shop.

Gift Tags: Gift tags are a dime a dozen at dollar stores during Christmas, but some people seek out custom gift tags on Etsy. Offering digital downloads of gift tag templates that can be customized by the user is a great niche for all special occasions and holidays, not just Christmas.

Gift tags can cover a variety of occasions and events, such as birthday gift tags, holiday gift tags, and themed gift tags. Gift tag sellers usually include multiple designs and color variations to allow users to choose their preferred design. By using digital downloads, users can access a wide range of gift tag designs quickly and easily from home. And since gift tag templates can be printed out multiple times, they save money over purchasing physical tags.

Once the gift tag template is downloaded, the customer can print the gift tags onto cardstock or other printable materials using their printer. They can then cut out the gift tags using scissors or a craft knife and use them to label and decorate their gifts. Many customers will further accentuate their tags with craft elements such as beads, stickers, or other decorations.

Greeting Cards: Greeting cards can include a variety of templates, such as traditional cards, modern cards, and themed cards for all occasions and holidays. Sellers can offer multiple designs and color variations to allow users to choose their preferred design as well as customization options.

Once the greeting card template is downloaded, the customer can print the cards onto cardstock and fold or cut them to their desired size. Some Etsy shops even offer envelope templates that can be downloaded along with the cards.

EDUCATION: With homeschooling, unschooling, tutoring, and virtual learning all becoming more commonplace, there has been a huge increase in the demand for educational digital downloads. Fortunately, you don't have to be an educator or parent to create and sell these items.

Workbooks: Workbooks are popular with parents, caregivers, and teachers who are looking for fun but educational activities for children. Digital download workbooks offer learning exercises for all ages and abilities. While the download isn't a physical book, some users will put the pages into binders to make their own "workbook." Others will simply use the sheets one at a time, printing out new copies as needed from the original download, making it more cost-effective than buying multiple workbooks for multiple kids.

Workbooks can include a variety of templates, such as math workbooks, reading comprehension workbooks, and writing practice workbooks. Once the workbook template is downloaded, the customer can easily print the pages onto whatever paper they choose.

Worksheets: While workbooks may contain multiple worksheets and exercises, a single worksheet is usually a stand-alone resource. Worksheets can include a variety of templates, such as math worksheets, grammar worksheets, and vocabulary worksheets.

Customers often search for worksheets to focus on a specific lesson or subject. Many Etsy shops that offer workbooks also include single worksheets for those that don't want an entire set. By including single pages along with sets, you can increase your product offerings to attract more shoppers.

Puzzles: Puzzles as digital downloads are pre-designed templates that provide users with a variety of puzzle games and challenges that can be printed and played from the convenience of one's home. These digital products can be downloaded and printed onto regular paper or special puzzle paper.

Puzzles can include a variety of templates, such as crossword puzzles, word search puzzles, Sudoku puzzles, and logic puzzles. They may also include multiple designs and difficulty levels to allow users to choose their preferred puzzle challenge. Note that if you sell puzzle sheets, you must also provide the answers to the puzzles. Often sellers will alternate the pages with the puzzle itself on the first page and the answers on the next page. Or they may separate the downloads into two separate files, with the puzzle sheets in one and the answers in another.

Many websites and software programs can be used to create puzzles. These tools can be a great resource for sellers who want to create high-quality, professional-looking puzzles to sell as digital downloads on Etsy. Here are some examples of websites and software programs that can be used to create puzzles:

- **Puzzle Maker:** This website allows users to create a variety of puzzles, including crossword puzzles, word search puzzles, and mazes.
- **Puzzle Baron:** This website offers a variety of puzzles and games, as well as a puzzle maker tool that allows users to create their puzzles.
- **Crossword Compiler:** This software program is designed specifically for creating crossword puzzles. It offers a range of features, including puzzle preview, clue editing, and grid customization.
- **The Puzzle Maker:** This software program allows users to create a variety of puzzles, including word search puzzles, Sudoku puzzles, and jigsaw puzzles.
- **Logic Puzzle Generator:** This website allows users to create logic puzzles, such as Sudoku and Kakuro puzzles.

Trivia: Trivia digital downloads provide users with a variety of trivia games and challenges that can be printed and played from the convenience of one's home or to take on trips. Trivia can include a variety of templates, such as general knowledge trivia, pop culture trivia, history trivia, and science trivia. They may also include multiple designs and difficulty levels to allow users to choose their preferred trivia challenge.

Note that sellers need to provide rules and answers for trivia downloads which allow customers to then play the game using the rules provided and check their answers using the answer key provided.

Also, remember that you cannot name your trivia games the same as trademarked brands such as Trivia Pursuit, Jeopardy, or any board game or game show. Copying any of these licensed product names, layouts or rules violates trademark laws. Therefore, you will need to create your unique games and rules.

Here are some steps you can follow to create trivia games:

1. **Choose a theme:** The first step in creating a trivia game is to choose a theme. You can choose a theme that interests you or one that you think will appeal to your target audience. Some popular themes include general knowledge, pop culture, history, science, and geography.
2. **Research the topic:** Once you have chosen a theme, you will need to research the topic to come up with questions for your trivia game. You can use books, websites, and other resources to gather information about the topic.
3. **Write the questions:** Based on your research, you can start writing the questions for your trivia game. Make sure the questions are interesting, challenging, and relevant to the

theme. You can also include multiple-choice options or fill-in-the-blank questions to make the game more engaging.

4. **Create the answer key:** Once you have written the questions, you will need to create an answer key that lists the correct answers. Make sure the answer key is accurate and easy to follow.

5. **Design the game:** Once you have written the questions and created the answer key, you can start designing the game. You can use software programs or websites to create a visually appealing and professional-looking trivia game. You can also add images or graphics to make the game more engaging.

6. **Test the game:** Before selling your trivia game as a digital download, it's a good idea to test the game with friends or family members to make sure it's fun, challenging, and well-designed. You can make any necessary changes or adjustments based on their feedback.

School Planners: It's not only adults who use planners. Kids of all ages need help organizing their schedules, classes, and homework assignments. School planners include pages for tracking important information such as class schedules, assignments, and deadlines, as well as sections for notetaking, goal setting, and reflection. They may also include motivational quotes or tips for academic success to help students stay motivated and focused.

School planner downloads are often put into binders by the user, making it easy to take out and add in pages. Plus having the pages as a digital file means the user can print out new pages if one is damaged or if they want to redo their writing. If you are selling other products geared towards children such as coloring and activity books, adding school planners into your shop is a great way to increase sales.

WEDDING: The wedding category is huge on Etsy. Customizable party favors, print-on-demand bridal party shirts, and bridal party gifts are all available on Etsy. When creating digital wedding products, note that many of the items are not in the standard 8.5" by 11" size and aren't meant for printer paper but rather come in a variety of sizes that the customer can print out on their own card stock.

Most sellers of wedding products include all or most of the following in their offerings so that the couple can coordinate all of their items:

Save The Date Cards: Save the Date cards are pre-wedding announcements that inform guests about the upcoming wedding date and location. They are typically sent out several months before the wedding to ensure that guests can reserve the date and make travel arrangements.

Save the Date cards are an excellent personalized digital product to sell on Etsy because they are affordable, easy to customize, and can be designed to match the couple's wedding theme. Sellers customize these cards according to the customer's preference. The buyer can easily download and print the cards onto their choice of card stock.

Bridal Party Invitations: Bridal Party invitations are a type of wedding invitations that are sent to invite bridesmaids, groomsmen, and other members of the bridal party to participate in the wedding festivities. These invitations are typically hand-delivered to each invitee after the couple has chosen their wedding date.

As a digital product, Bridal Party invitations are usually personalized by the seller according to the customer's direction. The buyer can then download the invitations and print them out onto their cardstock.

Bridal Shower Invitations: Bridal shower invitations are a type of invitation sent to invite guests to a pre-wedding celebration in honor of the bride-to-be. Bridal showers are usually organized by the maid of honor or a close family member and can be held at a venue or in someone's home.

As a digital product, bridal shower invitations are usually customized by the seller according to the customers' specifications.

Being able to print out as many invitations as the customer wants makes digital invites much more affordable than buying a set of invitations at the store. And in this day and age, some people choose to send invitations digitally, which means sellers need to make sure their files are suitable for both printing and emailing.

Wedding Invitations: Wedding invitations are formal invitations sent to invite guests to a wedding ceremony and reception. They are typically sent out several months in advance to allow guests enough time to make travel arrangements and RSVP. Wedding invitations are an essential part of the wedding planning process and are often the first impression that guests have of the wedding.

Wedding invitations are a popular digital product to sell on Etsy because they offer a wide range of customization options and can be designed to match the couple's wedding theme and color scheme. As a digital product, wedding invitations are personalized by the seller according to the customers' direction. They are a more affordable option than having custom invites printed.

Etsy sellers who specialize in wedding stationery typically offer a variety of designs, ranging from traditional and formal to modern and whimsical, to cater to different tastes and preferences. They also usually offer coordinating products, such as RSVP cards, thank-you cards, and wedding programs, to create a cohesive and memorable wedding experience for the couple and their guests.

Menus: Reception menus are another part of wedding stationery that lists the food and drink options that will be served at the wedding reception. They are usually placed at each table setting or displayed near the buffet or food stations.

As a digital product, reception menus are personalized by the seller and then downloaded and printed by the customer onto whatever paper they choose, making them a practical and cost-effective option for couples who want to create beautiful menus without the added expense of printing and shipping.

Etsy sellers who specialize in wedding stationery offer a variety of designs, ranging from simple and elegant to bold and colorful, to cater to different wedding themes and styles. They can also offer coordinating products, such as place cards and table numbers, to create a cohesive and polished look for the reception.

GRAPHIC DESIGN: While this book is mainly focused on beginner-level digital downloads and printables, if you are an experienced graphic designer, there are numerous digital products you can create and sell on Etsy. Because graphic design requires a higher skill set, there is less competition in this category and you can charge more for your products. Niches in graphic design include:

- **Lightroom Presents**
- **Procreate Brushes**
- **Printable Wall Art**

- **Photoshop Actions**
- **Clip Art**
- **Fonts**
- **Logos**
- **Video Intros**
- **Video Effects**
- **Photography**
- **Zoom Backgrounds**

Research: Hopefully the digital download ideas we've touched on have helped you narrow in on a category you want to focus on. However, if you are feeling overwhelmed, that's normal. After all, you probably didn't know there were so many digital products you could sell. And while you want to offer products that you enjoy creating, it's also important to research the market to see what customers are buying.

Here are some tips for researching the digital product market:

1. **Look at best-selling products:** One way to get an idea of what types of digital downloads are popular on Etsy is to look at the best-selling products in each category. This can give you an idea of what types of products are in high demand and what niches might be underserved.

2. **Browse competitor shops:** Another way to research digital downloads on Etsy is to browse the shops of competitors or

similar sellers in your chosen category. This can help you get a sense of what types of products are being sold, what pricing strategies are being used, and what types of customer reviews and feedback are being received. You never, even want to copy someone else's work but instead find inspiration in how you could offer products that fill a niche not currently being served.

3. **Use keyword research tools:** Keyword research tools can help you identify the most popular search terms and phrases related to your chosen category or niche. This can help you optimize your listings for search and improve your chances of being found by potential customers. I use **EtsyCheck.com** and **eRank.com**.

4. **Join Etsy forums and groups:** Etsy forums and groups can be a great resource for learning more about the market for digital downloads on Etsy. Note, however, that these groups can sometimes be a place where the competition lurks to steal ideas from successful sellers. I always find it best to simply read the discussions in these groups rather than participate.

5. **Watch YouTube videos:** There are thousands of YouTube videos dedicated to selling digital products. While many of these channels are also trying to sell courses and products related to the industry, they can be a good source of

information. However, take advice about what sells with a grain of salt. The fact is that as soon as someone makes a video saying they've found the next best seller, hundreds of other people who also watched the video are now going to make that product. Use YouTube for inspiration, not blind direction.

Choosing Your Niche: You may be thinking that you don't need to focus on a specific niche. After all, isn't it better to just create as many products as possible in your shop to reach the most people? Focusing on a specific niche when selling on Etsy is important for several reasons, the first of which is that it separates you from the competition. By focusing on a specific niche, you can differentiate yourself from competitors and establish a unique selling proposition. This can help them stand out in a crowded marketplace and attract customers who are specifically interested in their products.

Next is establishing expertise. When you focus on a specific niche, it allows you to develop expertise and knowledge in that chosen area. This can help you create the highest possible quality products that meet the specific needs of your target customers. After all, why would someone buy their wedding invitations from a shop that also sells sewing patterns for doll clothing and adult coloring pages?

Focusing on a specific niche also allows you to be more efficient as it enables you to streamline your operations and create more high-quality products in a shorter amount of time. If you are trying to create planners and then coloring books and then wedding save-the-date cards on the same day, you'll become flustered and the quality of your products may suffer. But if you focus on one product, say printable sticker sheets, you can reuse the same template with new graphics, making the creation and listing process go by much faster. The faster you can create new products, the faster you can build your shop. And the more products in your shop, the more potential customers you can reach.

All of this focus on choosing a niche is what will help you build a brand. And building a brand on Etsy is crucial to your success. Etsy is a highly competitive marketplace. Sellers who can narrow in on a niche and become the go-to shop for those particular products will succeed over those who spread themselves too thin. Narrowing in on a niche and putting up the highest quality products you are capable of will help you build a loyal customer base, generate repeat business, and establish a long-term presence in the marketplace.

Oh, and it will help you make the most money!

CHAPTER TWO: WHAT YOU NEED TO CREATE DIGITAL PRODUCTS

Hopefully, by now you have an idea of the types of digital products you want to sell on Etsy. But now you need to know what equipment and software you need to create those products. And you need to know what skills you'll need to produce high-quality items for your shop. As I'll mention several times throughout this book, selling digital products on Etsy is highly competitive. To stand out, you need to offer great-looking products.

The good news is that the investment to start a digital product business is very low. There is no inventory to buy, no shipping supplies to purchase, and since everything is done on the computer, you can work from anywhere. In fact, it's likely you already have most of the things necessary to start creating and selling digital products.

Computer: A computer is the one essential piece of equipment needed for this business. All of your work will be done on a computer. Whether it's a Mac or a PC, a desktop or a laptop is up to your personal preference. Most computers can be used for an Etsy digital download shop, as long as they meet the basic system requirements for the software and tools that you plan to use. You should be able to start your business using the computer you already have.

If you don't have a computer or are looking to upgrade, here are some general guidelines to consider when choosing a computer for your Etsy digital product shop:

Operating System: Etsy digital download shops can be operated on both Windows and Mac operating systems. Choose a computer that you are comfortable with and that supports the software tools you plan to use. I've used both Macs and PCs for my business. I currently use a Dell laptop but also utilize an Apple iPhone for some aspects of my business.

Both Windows and Mac operating systems will work just fine for a digital download business. It ultimately comes down to personal preference and which operating system you are most comfortable using. However, if you are buying a new system, there are some considerations to keep in mind when choosing an operating system for your digital download business:

1. **Software compatibility:** Make sure the software tools you plan to use are compatible with the operating system you choose. For example, some software may only be available on one operating system or may have different features or functionality depending on the operating system. Most graphic designers prefer to use Apple products. However, if

you plan to purchase ready-made graphics, a PC will work just fine.

2. **User interface:** The user interface of the operating system may vary between Windows and Mac, so consider which interface you prefer and find easiest to use. Again, it's really about personal preference. If you are happy with your current system, there is no reason to switch to a different one.

3. **Price:** Mac computers tend to be more expensive than Windows computers, so consider your budget and whether the added cost is worth it for your business needs. Again, Apple products are favored by graphic designers. I don't design my graphics; rather, I purchase ready-made graphics from other designers. Therefore, a PC works just fine for me.

Processor: An important consideration when creating digital products is needing a computer that can handle all of the files you will be saved to your system. Therefore, a computer with a fast and reliable processor will allow you to work more efficiently and handle larger files and applications. The processor is responsible for performing calculations, executing instructions, and managing data flow within the computer. A faster and more powerful processor will help you create and upload products to your Etsy shop quickly.

Memory: Computer memory, also known as RAM (Random Access Memory), is another important component for a digital download business. RAM is responsible for temporarily storing data and instructions that the processor needs to access quickly. The more RAM your computer has, the more programs and data it can keep in memory at once, which can improve overall performance and speed.

Storage: You will need enough storage space on your computer to store your digital files and other data. You will also want to consider using an external hard drive to store backups and additional files. Computer storage is a big component of a digital download business as it affects the amount of space available on your computer to store files and data. The more files you have on your system, the slower it will run. In my opinion, your system can never have too much storage!

Display: A high-quality display will improve your productivity and make it easier to work on detailed designs and graphics. The display is an important component of a computer for a digital download business. It is the interface between you and your computer and is responsible for displaying your digital products and other content.

When choosing a display for your digital download business, consider the following:

1. **Size:** The size of the display is measured diagonally in inches. Choose a size that meets your needs and fits your

workspace. A larger display can improve productivity and allow you to view multiple windows and programs at once.

2. **Resolution:** The resolution of the display is measured in pixels and determines the clarity and detail of the image. Choose a resolution that is appropriate for your needs and the type of digital products you will be creating and selling.

3. **Color accuracy:** Color accuracy is important for digital products that rely on color, such as graphics and designs. Choose a display with accurate color reproduction and calibration tools.

4. **Panel technology:** There are three main types of display panel technology: twisted nematic (TN), in-plane switching (IPS), and vertical alignment (VA). IPS displays are generally preferred for their superior color accuracy and viewing angles.

5. **Connectivity:** Make sure the display is compatible with your computer's graphics card and has the necessary connectivity ports, such as HDMI or DisplayPort.

Internet Connection: A reliable internet connection is vital for uploading and downloading large digital files and managing your Etsy shop. Your internet connectivity is a necessary component for a digital product business. After all, if you can't access the internet, you can't list your products on Etsy.

Software: Depending on the type of digital products you are selling, you may need software programs such as Adobe Creative Suite, Canva, or Microsoft Office to create and edit your designs. If, like me, you plan to purchase ready-made graphics from designers, you likely won't need to add software to your system beyond Microsoft Word as all other programs are available to use online without downloading them to your computer.

Design software, such as Adobe Illustrator or Photoshop, is essential for creating digital products such as graphics, designs, and patterns. If you plan to create your own graphics, then this type of software is essential. Most sellers who make their graphics use a combination of an iPad, Apple Pencils, and a software program such as Illustrator or Photoshop.

Productivity software, such as Microsoft Office or Google Docs, can be used to create business-related documents. Microsoft is essential for virtually every business, and for a digital product business, having Word installed on your computer will be a necessity. An email account will be needed to create an Etsy account. Most sellers, including myself, use Google for @gmail addresses. You can create as many email addresses as you want to through Google, which makes setting up a dedicated business email for your business easy.

Printer: If you are selling printable products that customers will need to print at home, you may need a printer to test your designs. Most digital downloads are black and white on 8.5" x 11" paper, which is fine for printing on standard printers. However, if you plan to sell highly detailed graphics (say, for wrapping paper or custom wedding invitations), you will want a high-quality color printer to test designs. You will also need to make sure customers understand the quality of the printer they will need to effectively print out their orders.

Cutting Machine: If you are selling products that customers will need to cut (for example, sticker sheets or die-cut signs), you may need to invest in a cutting machine to test your measurements. Note that if you do sell these types of products you will need to provide your customers with the measurements and instructions for them to print and cut the final product on their end. Cricut is the top selling of these machines.

External Hard Drive: It's a good idea to have an external hard drive to back up your digital files and keep them organized. Graphic files are especially taxing on computer systems, so saving your files to an external hard drive will not only free up space on your system but it will also keep your computer running fast.

Graphics Subscriptions: Unless you plan to design all of your graphics and products completely yourself, you are going to need to purchase graphics and even page layouts for your business. Fortunately, there are numerous options available to access the tools necessary to easily create products. These include:

Tangent Templates: Tangent Templates is a software program designed specifically for creating printables and digital products. It provides a range of tools and features that can help sellers on Etsy create high-quality, professional-looking digital products to sell in their shops.

With Tangent Templates, sellers can create a variety of digital products, including planners, journals, calendars, and more. The software provides a range of templates and design elements that can be customized to create unique and visually appealing products.

Note that you cannot sell the templates offered on Tangent Templates as is. For example, you can't download one of their planner templates and list it as-is on Etsy. You will need to edit the images in some way by adding text or graphics.

Some of the key features of Tangent Templates include:

- **Easy-to-use interface:** The software is designed with an intuitive, user-friendly interface that makes it easy to create digital products quickly and efficiently.
- **Templates and design elements:** Tangent Templates provides a range of templates and design elements that can

be customized to create unique products. These include pre-designed layouts, graphics, fonts, and more.

- **Customizable colors and branding:** Sellers can customize the colors and branding of their digital products to match their brand or business.
- **Export to PDF and other file formats:** Tangent Templates allows sellers to export their digital products in a range of file formats, including PDF, JPEG, and PNG, making it easy to upload and sell on Etsy.
- **Extensive help and tutorials:** Tangent Templates has an active YouTube channel and Facebook group where you can get help and support.

Tangent Templates is a one-time paid subscription. You can learn more at https://templates.tangent.rocks/.

BookBolt: BookBolt is similar to Tangent Templates in that it is another software program designed specifically for creating printables and digital products to sell on online marketplaces such as Etsy. The software offers a range of tools and features that can help sellers create high-quality, professional-looking digital products quickly and efficiently.

Note that you cannot sell the templates offered on BookBolt as is. Just as explained earlier with Tangent Templates, you can't download one of BookBolt's planner templates and list it as-is on

Etsy. You will need to edit the images in some way by adding text or graphics.

Some of the key features of BookBolt include:

- **Templates and design elements:** BookBolt provides a range of templates and design elements that can be customized to create unique digital products. These include pre-designed layouts, graphics, fonts, and more.
- **Customizable colors and branding:** Sellers can customize the colors and branding of their digital products to match their brand or business.
- **Keyword research and optimization:** BookBolt offers keyword research and optimization tools to help sellers create products that are optimized for search and have a better chance of being found by potential customers.
- **Image editing tools:** BookBolt provides image editing tools that allow sellers to enhance and edit their images, add text overlays, and create custom graphics.
- **Sales analytics:** BookBolt offers sales analytics that allows sellers to track the performance of their digital products, monitor sales trends, and identify growth opportunities.

BookBolt is a paid yearly subscription service. You can learn more online at https://bookbolt.io/.

Tangent Templates vs. BookBolt: So, which is better: Tangent Templates or BookBolt? It honestly comes down to personal preference. I use both for creating journals, planners, and coloring book pages. Both offer several pre-made pages as well as the ability to create pages from scratch. Tangent Template offers more support with its YouTube channel and Facebook group, while BookBolt has more templates including some that are completely free.

I recommend checking out Tangent Templates on YouTube and Facebook to see examples of their products. And I recommend creating a free account with BookBolt to see the free products they offer before deciding if you want to pay for a subscription.

Canva: Canva is a popular graphic design software that can be used to create high-quality digital products. Canva offers a range of features and tools that can help sellers create unique and visually appealing products quickly and efficiently.

Here are some ways that sellers of digital products can utilize Canva:

- **Design templates:** Canva offers a wide range of design templates that sellers can use to create digital products such as planners, journals, calendars, and more. These templates can be customized with unique branding and content to create unique products.

- **Custom graphics:** Canva provides a range of design elements such as icons, illustrations, and stock photos that can be used to create custom graphics for digital products.
- **Text overlays:** Canva allows sellers to add text overlays to their designs, including custom fonts, colors, and styles.
- **Branding elements:** Canva allows sellers to upload and save branding elements such as logos, colors, and fonts to ensure consistent branding across all digital products.
- **Export options:** Canva provides a range of export options for digital products, including PDF, PNG, and JPEG formats.

Canva has a free version, but if you are planning on using any of their graphics, elements, or fonts in digital products to sell, you will need to upgrade to the paid **Canva Pro** subscription, which gives you the license to use their images in a print-on-demand business. You can pay monthly or save money by paying for a year upfront. To learn more, visit https://www.canva.com/.

Creative Fabrica: Creative Fabrica is the most popular marketplace for digital products, including fonts, graphics, and design templates. Sellers of digital downloads can use Creative Fabrica in several ways, including:

- **Selling digital products:** Sellers can upload their digital products to Creative Fabrica's marketplace and sell them directly to customers. Creative Fabrica takes care of payment processing and provides sellers with access to a large customer base.

- **Marketing and promotion:** Creative Fabrica offers a range of marketing and promotion tools for sellers, including featured listings, email campaigns, and social media promotions.
- **Product creation:** Sellers can use Creative Fabrica's design resources, such as fonts and graphics, to create new digital products to sell on their own websites or other marketplaces.
- **Collaborations:** Sellers can collaborate with other designers and creators on Creative Fabrica to create new digital products or promote each other's products.
- **Learning and resources:** Creative Fabrica offers a range of learning resources, including tutorials and courses, to help sellers improve their skills and grow their businesses.

Most digital product sellers use Creative Fabrica to purchase graphics to use in their designs. For example, you can buy coloring book pages on Creative Fabrica that you can then alter in Canva Pro. Just as you can't sell the templates from Tangent Templates and BookBolt as-is, you cannot sell the designs you download from Creative Fabrica unless you alter them in some way.

The most important thing you need to remember when using graphics from Creative Fabrica is to make sure the designs have the

Print on Demand license. This license allows you to use the graphics on items you plan to sell. Without this license, you open yourself up to having the designer file a claim against your listing, resulting in Etsy removing your listing and maybe even suspending your account.

You can subscribe to Creative Fabrica on a monthly or yearly basis. To learn more, visit https://www.creativefabrica.com/.

While Tangent Templates, BookBolt, Canva, and Creative Fabrica are the most popular websites used to create digital products, there are some others that you may want to look at:

- **PicMonkey** is a photo editing and design tool that can be used to create digital products such as graphics, social media posts, and printables.
- **Adobe Creative Cloud** is a suite of design software programs, including Photoshop, Illustrator, and InDesign, that can be used to create a wide range of digital products.
- **Affinity Designer** is a vector graphics software program that can be used to create digital products such as logos, illustrations, and icons.
- **Silhouette Studio** is a software program that can be used to design and create digital products such as cutting files, printables, and decals. 5. Procreate: Procreate is a digital painting and illustration app that can be used to create

digital products such as custom illustrations, digital art, and graphics.

My Way: I am not a graphic designer. I cannot draw or create designs from scratch. However, I've been selling digital products for years. I use Tangent Templates to create book interiors for planners and journals that I publish as books on Amazon. I purchase graphics from Creative Fabrica, such as coloring book pages, and edit them in Canva Pro to create downloadable files to sell on Etsy. I've also utilized Microsoft Word to create basic text templates for various businesses.

If, like me, you aren't a graphic designer, don't let that stop you from starting a digital product business. The fact is that most digital product sellers on Etsy are NOT designing their products from scratch but rather utilizing the programs mentioned above. As long as you are paying for the subscriptions and are following the rules laid out by each, you can use these programs to create products that will sell on Etsy.

CHAPTER THREE: CREATING DIGITAL PRODUCTS

So far, we've discussed the different types of digital products you can sell, along with the various categories and niches. And we've covered the equipment and software necessary to start an Etsy shop selling digital products. Now comes the fun part: Creating your products!

As noted in the previous chapter, exactly what programs you will need to create digital products will depend on the type of items you want to sell. Since this is a beginner's guide book, we'll be focusing on the easiest printable items that almost anyone can create. And since most sellers use either Tangent Templates, BookBolt, and/or Canva Pro along with Creative Fabrica, the examples listed in this chapter will use those tools.

The one thing you need to focus on is that whatever printable product you are creating needs to be a PDF file.

A PDF file, or Portable Document Format file, is a type of file format that is commonly used for documents and files that need to be shared or printed. PDF files are designed to be compatible with a wide range of devices and operating systems. That means I can create a PDF on my PC and email it to you for you to download on your Mac.

Key features of PDF files are:

1. **Compatibility:** PDF files can be opened and viewed on a wide range of devices and operating systems, including smartphones, tablets, computers, and e-readers.

2. **Security:** PDF files can be encrypted to prevent unauthorized access or modification. This makes them a popular option for digital products as unless you enable your items to be edited, no one can alter them.

3. **Printability:** PDF files are designed to be printable, which means that they can be printed out on a wide range of printers without losing quality or formatting.

4. **File size:** PDF files can be relatively small in size, which makes them easy to share and distribute over the internet.

As an Etsy digital download seller, you will be creating PDF files that you will then list on Etsy. When a customer buys one of your digital downloads, Etsy will facilitate transferring the PDF file to your customer. The customer will then download the file onto their own computer system and print it out themselves.

Creating a PDF file may sound difficult, but it is quite easy. Tangent Templates, BookBolt, and Canva make all of their products available as PDF files. And most sellers on Creative Fabrica do, too.

Microsoft Word: But what if you don't want to invest in those software programs? If you have Microsoft Word, you can easily create a PDF of any Word document:

1. Open your document in Microsoft Word.
2. Click on the "File" tab and then click "Save As".
3. Choose a location to save the file and then select "PDF" as the file type.
4. Click "Save" to create the PDF file.

Alternatively, you can also use the "Export" function in Microsoft Word to create a PDF file:

1. Open your document in Microsoft Word.
2. Click on the "File" tab and then click "Export".
3. Choose a location to save the file and then select "PDF" as the file type.
4. Click "Export" to create the PDF file.

There are many types of digital downloads that you can create in Microsoft Word and then save as a PDF file to sell on Etsy. Here are some examples:

Planners: You can create basic daily, weekly, monthly, or yearly planners using Microsoft Word and then save them as PDF files. Here is a general process for creating a planner in Microsoft Word:

1. Open a new document in Microsoft Word and set the page orientation to portrait mode.
2. Create a table: In the "Insert" tab, select "Table", and then choose the number of rows and columns you want to use for your planner. You can adjust the size of the table by clicking and dragging the edges.
3. Add headings: Add headings to your planner by typing in the column and row headers. For example, you could have columns for "Date," "To-Do," "Notes," and "Goals."
4. Format the table: Use the table formatting tools to adjust the size, color, and font of the table and headings. You can also add borders and shading to make the planner more visually appealing.
5. Add content: Start adding content to your planner by filling in the cells with dates, to-do lists, notes, and other relevant information. Make sure the content is organized and easy to read.
6. Add graphics and other design elements: To make your planner more visually appealing, you can add graphics such as icons, patterns, and borders. You can also add your branding elements such as your logo and color scheme.
7. Save the document: Once you have finished designing your planner, save the document and then export it as a PDF file.

To do this, click on "File," then "Save As," and then choose "PDF" as the file type.

The same process used to create planner pages in Word can also be used for other products such as worksheets and budget trackers.

Invitations: You can create digital invitations for events such as weddings, birthdays, and holidays in Word. Note that these products will need to be personalized to the customer's specifications. You'll want to create a general invitation and then personalize it once an order is placed. Here's how to do that:

1. Open a new document in Microsoft Word and set the page orientation to portrait mode.
2. Choose a template: Microsoft Word offers a variety of pre-designed templates that you can choose from. Go to the "File" menu and select "New," then type "invitations" into the search bar to see the available options.
3. Customize the template: Once you have selected a template, you can customize it by changing the text, font, and color scheme to fit your needs. You can also add your own images or graphics to the design.
4. Download this file and list it for sale on Etsy. But keep it as a Word document on your computer.
5. Add event details: Once a customer has placed an order and provided you with their details, go to your computer and

open the Word document. Add the event details such as the date, time, location, and RSVP information to the invitation.

6. Finalize the design: Once you have added all the necessary information, take a moment to review the invitation and make any final tweaks or adjustments to the design.

7. Save the document as a PDF file by going to the "File" menu and selecting "Save As," then choosing "PDF" as the file type.

8. Go to Etsy and finalize sending the updated PDF to your customer.

Greeting Cards: Greeting cards for special occasions and holidays are another digital download you can create in Microsoft Word. Here's how:

1. Open a new document in Microsoft Word and set the page orientation to landscape mode.

2. Choose a template: Microsoft Word offers a variety of pre-designed templates that you can choose from. Go to the "File" menu and select "New," then type "greeting cards" into the search bar to see the available options.

3. Customize the template: Once you have selected a template, you can customize it by changing the text, font, and color scheme to fit your needs. You can also add your own images or graphics to the design.

4. Save the document as a PDF file by going to the "File" menu and selecting "Save As," then choosing "PDF" as the file type.
5. List the PDF for sale on Etsy.

Resumes & Cover Letters: Resumes and cover letters are two popular yet very easy digital products to create in Word to then sell on Etsy. You can create basic templates that customers fill in with their own information, or you can enter their information for them. As with invitations and greeting cards, Word has templates for resumes and cover letters that you can use. Make sure to edit the templates and add new elements to differentiate yours from the others being sold on Etsy.

Books: You can utilize Microsoft Word to create books and then convert them to PDF files for sale on Etsy. In fact, the book you are currently reading was originally written in Microsoft Word and later formatted for sale on Amazon as both a Kindle e-book and a paperback.

When offering books for sale on Etsy, it's important to focus on shorter reads such as instructions, guides, recipes, or single-topic educational materials. For example, if you are selling digital workbooks or activities for kids, you may want to write instructional booklets that complement the topics covered in the workbooks.

Any book you upload for sale online must be original work created by you. Plagiarizing someone else's work, republishing books written by others, and selling single chapters from other people's books are not allowed. Not only will your listing get taken down by Etsy, but you also risk losing your Etsy account. And even more serious, you may face legal repercussions for plagiarism.

So, why not simply build a business by creating digital downloads in Microsoft Word? Well, Microsoft Word is rather limiting in terms of layout and design features. While you can certainly create digital products in Microsoft Word, and while it can be a good place to start, if you want to make more sophisticated products with less effort, using some of the programs we've already discussed will give you more options.

For example, instead of creating planner pages in Word, you can create them using Tangent Templates or BookBolt, both of which have planner pages with dates, grids, and other features already laid out. Or you can use Canva Pro to alter their planner page templates. You can also purchase planner templates from Creative Fabrica and upload the files to Canva to edit and add elements.

Here's an example of how I've created a PDF of adult coloring pages that I sold as a digital download on Etsy:

1. I searched Creative Fabrica for coloring book pages and downloaded the ones I liked, making sure they had the Print on Demand license.
2. I created an 8.5" x 11" page in Canva Pro.
3. I uploaded the graphics I downloaded from Creative Fabrica to Canva.
4. I then inserted the graphics one by one into individual pages.
5. I edited the images and added other design elements to make my pages different from other sellers who may have purchased the same graphics.
6. Once I was happy with my pages, I downloaded them as a PDF file to my computer.
7. I then uploaded that PDF file to a new Etsy listing.
8. When someone purchased my coloring pages, Etsy transferred the file to the customer and, after deducting their fees, deposited the remaining balance into my account.

PRO TIP: A lot of Etsy sellers use Creative Fabrica for digital downloads. When I am searching the site for graphics, I sort by "newest" first. This way I see the newest uploads, the ones that other sellers haven't started using yet. I also select the Print on Demand license to ensure I am only seeing images that I can use in designs I plan to sell.

After I've selected a graphic, I then make sure to alter the image in some way. As noted above, when I'm creating coloring pages, I will use images from Creative Fabrica but I then edit them or add elements to them in Canva Pro. One thing I like to do is create a border around the image. I may add in text, crop part of the design out, or add in graphics using my Canva Pro subscription. Remember that you need the Canva Pro subscription to use their elements on anything you plan to sell.

While other sellers may have purchased the same graphics from Creative Fabric that I also use, I do my best to edit them to make them as unique as possible.

Tangent Templates & BookBolt: Both Tangent Templates and BookBolt provide a wealth of options for creating high-quality digital downloads. However, as already noted, it's important to remember that simply taking the pre-made templates they offer and selling them as digital downloads as-is not allowed. Instead, you need to alter them in some way. Both platforms offer customization features to help you turn their ready-made templates into your own custom creations.

For instance, Tangent Templates provides calendar and planner pages that you can customize with dates, fonts, and sidebars, among several other options. With this software, you can also create custom guided journal pages that include your own unique questions on each page. You can then import those pages into another section of the site where you can add graphic elements.

Similarly, BookBolt offers a range of customizable templates for creating e-books, workbooks, and other digital products. You can add your own text, images, and design elements to pre-made templates to create unique products. Additionally, BookBolt's optimization features help ensure that your products are properly formatted for sale on various online marketplaces, including Etsy.

You can also download the templates from both Tangent and BookBolt and edit them in Canva. Plus, you can even add elements you purchased from Creative Fabrica to your products, creating truly unique items that no one else is selling.

Canva: By subscribing to Canva Pro, you gain access to an extensive library of designs, templates, colors, and fonts that can be used to create digital downloads for your Etsy shop. Whether you're looking to create printable planners, social media templates, or marketing materials, Canva Pro provides a wealth of options to choose from. In fact, with the wide range of features available in Canva Pro, you can use it as your go-to tool for creating all of your digital products from start to finish without investing in any other software or subscribing to any other programs.

Remember that you need to pay for a Canva Pro subscription to use any of their design elements in products you plan to sell. Here are some examples of digital products that you can create using Canva Pro:

- **Printable planners and organizers:** Canva offers a wide range of planner templates that you can customize with your own images, fonts, and colors. You can create daily, weekly, monthly, and yearly planners, as well as specialized planners for specific topics such as fitness, meal planning, and budgeting.

- **Social media templates:** Canva has a variety of templates that you can use to create eye-catching social media graphics for platforms such as Instagram, Facebook, and Twitter. These templates are pre-designed and can be easily customized with your own branding and messaging.

- **Marketing materials:** Canva provides a range of templates for marketing materials such as brochures, flyers, business cards, and posters. These templates are fully customizable, allowing you to add your own images and text to create professional-looking marketing materials for your Etsy shop.

- **Invitations and cards:** Canva has a variety of templates for invitations, greeting cards, and other types of cards that you can customize for your Etsy shop. These templates can be easily personalized with your own images and text, making it easy to create unique and personalized cards for your customers.

- **E-books and guides:** Canva also provides templates for e-books and guides, which you can use to create digital products such as e-books, guides, and workbooks. These templates are designed to be easy to use and can be customized with your own images, text, and branding.

Here's a step-by-step guide on how to create digital products in Canva Pro:

1. **Choose a template:** Canva offers a wide range of templates that you can use as a starting point for your digital products. To find a template, click on the "Templates" button on the left-hand side of the screen and browse through the available options. Once you've found a template you like, click on it to open it in the editor.

2. **Customize the template:** Once you've opened the template in the editor, you can customize it to fit your needs. This may include adding your own images, changing the colors and fonts, and adjusting the layout.

3. **Save your design:** Once you're happy with your design, click on the "Download" button in the top right-hand corner of the screen. From here, you can choose to download your design as a PDF or JPG file.

4. **Upload your product to Etsy:** Once you've finished editing your PDF, you can upload it to Etsy as a digital product.

Creative Fabrica: Although Tangent Templates, BookBolt, and Canva offer customization options to create unique digital downloads, Creative Fabrica works a bit differently. With Creative Fabrica, you are purchasing pre-made designs that are already complete and ready to be used.

However, when it comes to selling these graphics as digital products, you must alter them first. You can't just sell the graphics as-is.

For example, I may purchase a graphic from Creative Fabrica that I use on one of my book covers. I don't have to alter it in any way because the product I am selling is the book, not the graphic. The graphic is just part of the cover. The product is the book itself.

However, when it comes to selling digital products, the graphics ARE the products. Therefore, you can't sell graphics you buy on Creative Fabrica to customers on Etsy who are buying graphics. You have to USE the graphic on a product. You also have to make sure the graphic has the Print on Demand license we've already discussed. And you'll need to enter Creative Fabrica as a Production Partner on Etsy. More on that later in this book.

Hiring a Designer: When it comes to creating digital downloads, you may find that you have the ideas but lack the ability, for whatever reason, to bring your products to life. If that is the case, you may want to hire a designer to help create professional PDF files for you to sell.

To hire a designer for your digital product business, you will first need to research online to find potential candidates. Freelancing platforms like Upwork and Fiverr can be a great place to find talented designers who specialize in creating digital products. Once you have found a few leads, you should review their portfolios to get a sense of their style and the quality of their work. It's important to choose a designer who has experience creating digital downloads similar to the products you want to sell on Etsy. And it's also important to ensure they aren't selling the same products they create for you to other sellers.

Hiring out every single product you want to create is costly. Therefore, you may want to only outsource the most complex products that you simply cannot make yourself.

Do What Works for You: While I use a variety of resources to create my digital products, it's certainly possible to focus on one or two tools that work best for your business needs. For example, you can customize your products using the templates available in programs like Word, Tangent Templates, BookBolt, or Canva. Alternatively, you can purchase pre-made templates from graphic sites like Creative Fabrica and edit them in Canva to make them unique to your brand. If you need additional assistance, you can also hire a designer through platforms like Fiverr or UpWork to help you bring your ideas to life.

With so many options available, it can be overwhelming to decide where to begin when creating digital downloads for your Etsy shop. If you're new to working with computers, start by exploring the features available in Word to create your products. For more advanced designs, consider watching tutorial videos on Tangent Templates' YouTube channel to learn how to utilize their website to create customized products. Additionally, you can start with the free version of Canva to get a feel for the site before committing to a Pro subscription. Look over the free templates available on BookBolt. And browse Creative Fabrica to see what is available there.

Remember, building a successful digital product shop on Etsy takes time and patience. Don't be discouraged if a product doesn't work out as planned – you can always choose not to list it or remove it from your shop if it doesn't sell. The key is to experiment, learn from your successes and failures, and continue to refine your offerings based on customer feedback and demand. With persistence and dedication, you can build a thriving Etsy shop selling digital downloads that customers love.

PRO TIP: Do you have an idea for a digital product but are lost as to how to create it? Chances are there is a YouTube tutorial available to watch! YouTube offers a wealth of FREE information when it comes to creating digital products. Simply type the name of the product you want to create into the YouTube search bar to find a step-by-step video on how to make it!

CHAPTER FOUR: OPENING AN ETSY SHOP

So far we've covered the different types of digital products you can create along with the various categories and niches there are. We've talked about the equipment and software you need for a digital product business, and we've discussed how to create these products. Now comes the next big step: Opening up your Etsy shop!

To sell on Etsy you need to create a seller account. If you already have an account as an Etsy shopper, a seller account is an added step. You will still have everything under one main account, but you will need to provide additional information for approval to sell products on Etsy. Once logged in, you can sell or buy. There's no need to log into two separate accounts.

To set up an Etsy seller account, follow these steps:

1. Go to the **Etsy website** and click on the **Sell on Etsy** button.
2. Click the **Open your Etsy shop** button.
3. Enter your **email address** and **password** to create an account or sign in with an existing account. You can create your seller account under your buyer account, you'll just need to add some additional information.
4. Choose your **shop language** and **country**.
5. Enter your **shop name.**
6. Agree to **Etsy's terms of use and policies.**

7. Click the **Create your shop** button to complete the process.

After you have finished the **Create Your Etsy Shop** process, you will next need to configure your **Shop Preferences.** This can be done through the **Shop Manager**, which is accessible through the store-shaped icon in your Etsy **Seller Dashboard** (it's located at the top of all Etsy pages). Note that you can skip this step and return later to set up your store. And you can modify your settings at any time in the future.

PRO TIP: I have my **Shop Manager** bookmarked on my desktop computer so that I can quickly access it to create new listings and manage my shop. I also have the **Etsy Seller App** installed on my phone so I can easily access my account from anywhere at any time. Being able to access my shop when I'm away from my office is important as it allows me to quickly answer any messages from buyers. Etsy is very strict about sellers answering questions from customers as quickly as possible; failing to do so in a timely manner can affect your seller status. So having the app allows me to respond to questions even when I am away from my office.

Etsy Shop Preferences are the settings that allow you to customize and manage various aspects of your Etsy shop. You can access your shop preferences by going to **Shop Manager** and clicking on the **Preferences** tab.

Here are some of the things you can do in your **Etsy Shop Preferences**:

- Set your shop location and language.
- Set your shop policies, such as your return policy.
- Customize your shop's appearance by adding a banner image, logo, and other branding elements.
- Enable automatic renewal for your listings.
- Choose how you want to handle orders, including setting up automatic email responses.
- Set up Google Analytics to track your shop's performance.
- Set up shipping profiles to streamline the process of shipping your products. While you won't be shipping digital products, if you are creating custom printables or digital files, you will want to set up your processing times.
- Enable or disable various features, such as the ability to offer gift wrapping or to allow customers to request custom orders. I recommend you do not allow returns on digital products simply because a buyer changed their mind. If there was a mistake within the file, you can easily correct it and sent the customer a new one.

Time Commitment: Etsy will ask you to indicate your *Time Commitment* to your shop. This question asks about your level of dedication as a seller, but it is not a determining factor in your eligibility to sell on Etsy or the success of your shop. You can choose to select whether selling on Etsy is your full-time or part-time job, or you can simply leave the question unanswered. The decision is entirely up to you and will only be used by Etsy for informational purposes.

Shop Name: Choosing a shop name is a crucial step in establishing your brand on Etsy. It's important to select a name that reflects the type of items you sell and is easy for customers to remember and spell. If you have a specific niche and already know what type of products you'll be offering, consider a name that aligns with that. However, be cautious of choosing a name that's too narrow as it may restrict you from expanding your product line as your shop grows. For instance, if you name your shop "Wedding Invitations," you may be limiting yourself if you decide to offer items such as save-the-date cards, bridal party invites, and reception menus in the future. Instead, consider a name like "Wonderous Weddings" that implies your niche while allowing room for growth.

While you can edit your shop name at any time, it is important to keep in mind that changing your shop name on Etsy can create confusion for your customers and may require you to update your branding elements and promotional campaigns, including changing your social media handles. Therefore, it is best to choose a shop name that you plan to keep from the beginning. Although Etsy does allow you to change your shop name, it's advisable not to after you start making significant sales.

You also need to make sure that your shop name adheres to Etsy's naming guidelines and that it doesn't contain any prohibited words or phrases. Etsy has certain requirements and guidelines for shop names to ensure that they are appropriate and do not violate the platform's policies. Here are some of the main requirements and guidelines for shop names on Etsy:

- Shop names must be unique and not already in use by another Etsy seller.
- Shop names must not contain any prohibited words or phrases, such as offensive language or trademarked terms.
- Shop names must not imply that you are affiliated with Etsy or any other company or organization.
- Shop names must not contain any personal information, such as phone numbers or addresses.
- Shop names must not be too long or difficult to spell or pronounce.
- Shop names must be 4-20 characters in length.
- Shop names cannot contain spaces or special characters.
- Shop names cannot contain profanity.

- Shop names are exclusive to one shop, meaning you can't create a shop name that is already being used by an existing Etsy member.
- Shop names cannot infringe on another's trademark.

Set Up Payment & Billing: In the next step of setting up your Etsy shop, you will be required to provide payment and billing information. This includes entering a valid payment method that Etsy can use to charge you in case your fees exceed your sales. Remember that when you sell anything on Etsy, whether it is a physical product or a digital download, Etsy will automatically take out their fees and shipping costs before depositing the remaining balance in your Etsy account. If you have to process a refund or if your fees exceed your net profits, your Etsy balance could fall into the negative. At that time, Etsy would charge your credit card for any outstanding fees you've occurred.

When setting up your Etsy shop, you will also need to specify a payment method so Etsy can pay you for your sales. To set up your Etsy shop's payment and billing, you will need to follow these steps:

1. Go to the **Shop Manager** and click on the **Finances** tab.
2. Click on the **P**ayment settings option.
3. Since your orders will be processed through Etsy, they choose the payment methods they accept.
4. Click the **Save** button to save your payment settings.

When creating an Etsy seller account, the information required may differ depending on whether you are registering as an individual/sole proprietorship or a business. As an individual/sole proprietor, you will need to provide personal information such as your name, contact information, and, if in the United States, your social security number. However, if you're registering a business, specifically an LLC, you will need to provide more detailed information about your business, such as its official name, contact information, and relevant documentation.

Are you confused about the difference between a sole proprietorship and an LLC? Don't worry, many new sellers are.

A **sole proprietorship** is a type of business entity in which an individual is the sole owner and operator of the business. As the sole proprietor, the owner has complete control over all aspects of the business and is personally responsible for all debts and liabilities. For tax purposes, the business is not considered a separate entity, and the owner reports all business income and expenses on their tax return. In the United States, a sole proprietor may use their Social Security number as their business identification number for tax purposes.

An **LLC** also offers greater flexibility in terms of taxation. By default, an LLC is considered a "pass-through" entity, which means that the profits and losses of the business pass through to the owners' personal tax returns, and the business itself does not pay federal income taxes. However, LLCs can choose to be taxed as a corporation if they prefer.

Additionally, an LLC can have an unlimited number of owners, unlike a sole proprietorship which is limited to one. In terms of legal requirements, an LLC typically requires more paperwork and formalities than a sole proprietorship. This can include filing articles of organization with the state, creating an operating agreement, and obtaining any necessary licenses or permits. However, the exact requirements vary by state.

When it comes to selling digital products on Etsy, both sole proprietorships and LLCs have advantages and disadvantages, and the appropriate choice for your business will depend on your specific needs and circumstances. It is always a good idea to consult with a legal or financial professional before deciding on the best business structure for your company.

Most Etsy sellers, including myself, are sole proprietors. As explained above, being a sole proprietor simply means that I pay taxes as an individual, not a corporation, using my social security number and not a business license. I operate my Etsy shop as a one-person business and am not registered as a corporation or LLC with the government. As a sole proprietorship, I pay taxes (in

America) as an individual using my social security number and do not need a business license.

That's right: As a sole proprietor, you typically do not need to file any type of paperwork with your city, state, or federal governments for your Etsy shop. Rather, you will simply be taxed as an individual. Again, this is the case for most places in America; please check with a tax professional or lawyer in your area to see what the requirements are where you live.

If you are registering as an individual/sole proprietorship on Etsy, you will need to provide specific information on the **How you'll get paid** page during the setup process of your shop, including:

- Your full legal name and contact information including address and phone number
- Your social security number (for United States citizens) or your taxpayer identification number (TIN)
- Your bank account information, including the bank name, routing number, and account number. You can find your routing and account numbers at the bottom of your checks.

Test Deposit: Once you have entered your payment and billing information on Etsy, they may conduct a verification process by issuing a small test deposit, less than a dollar, to your bank account or PayPal account. This is standard practice to ensure that your payment information is correct and that you will be able to receive payouts from Etsy. You are not required to pay back the test deposit. To complete the verification process, you will need to check your bank account or PayPal account to locate the test deposit and confirm its receipt. Finally, you enter the amount of the test deposit on the "How you'll get paid" page to complete the verification process.

The test deposit may take a few days to appear in your account, so be sure to check back periodically if you do not see it right away. If you have any issues with the verification process, you can contact Etsy's support team for assistance. You can easily contact Etsy support at any time and for any reason by following these steps:

1. Go to **www.etsy.com** and click the **Help & Policies** tab at the bottom of the page.
2. Scroll down to the **Contacting Etsy** section and click the **Contact Us** button.
3. Select the appropriate **category** for your issue from the dropdown menu.
4. Enter a **subject** and a **detailed description** of your issue in the provided fields.
5. Click the **Continue** button to submit your request.

Etsy support typically responds within 24 hours, although it can take longer during peak times.

Two-Factor Authentication: Two-factor authentication is an additional security measure that requires you to provide a verification code when signing in from an unrecognized browser or device. This helps to protect your account from unauthorized access and ensures that only you can access your Etsy shop.

To set up two-factor authentication, you will need to choose a method for receiving your verification code. Etsy allows you to receive your verification code in one of three ways:

1. **Text message:** If you choose this option, you will receive a text message with your verification code whenever you need to sign in from an unrecognized browser or device.
2. **Authenticator app:** If you choose this option, you will need to download an authenticator app on your phone and use it to generate your verification code whenever you need to sign in from an unrecognized browser or device.
3. **Email:** If you choose this option, you will receive an email with your verification code whenever you need to sign in from an unrecognized browser or device.

Set Up Your Storefront: Once you've gotten through entering your personal and banking information, verifying your account, and setting up two-factor authorization, you can move on to setting up your Etsy shop storefront!

To set up your Etsy shop storefront, follow these steps (note that we'll go over these options more in-depth later in this chapter):

1. Go to your Etsy seller dashboard and click the **Shop settings** tab.
2. Click the **Shop info & Appearance** tab on the left side of the page.
3. Enter a **shop title** and **shop announcement** that will appear at the top of your shop's homepage.
4. Add a **shop banner** image that will appear at the top of your shop's homepage.
5. Add a **shop icon**, which is a small image that will represent your shop on Etsy.
6. Enter a **shop description** that will appear on your shop's homepage and in search results.
7. Click the **Save** button to save your changes.

Etsy Standard: *Etsy Standard* is the default level of shop access for all sellers on the platform. It offers fundamental features and functions necessary for starting to sell on Etsy. This package enables sellers to create a seller account, which, in turn, generates an Etsy shop and allows them to list items for sale.

With *Etsy Standard,* sellers can personalize their shop page to reflect their product offerings. There is no additional charge to open an Etsy shop; the only price is the listing fee of $0.20 per item, charged when you create a new listing or relist an expired one. This fee remains valid for four months.

To edit your Etsy Shop, first, log into your **Shop Manager**. Then **click on the pencil icon next to your shop's name**. This will bring up a page where you can edit your shop's banner, icon, and featured items area.

Etsy Plus: *Etsy Plus* is a premium subscription service that provides sellers with advanced features and tools beyond what is included in the basic *Etsy Standard* plan. For a monthly fee of $10, *Etsy Plus* members receive 15 credits to promote their listings through Promoted Listings and Etsy Ads programs, as well as an additional $5 credit for Etsy Ads.

In addition to these advertising benefits, *Etsy Plus* subscribers get access to advanced shop appearance options, a custom domain name, and Etsy's wholesale platform. Moreover, *Etsy Plus* offers a discount on Hover domains, although sellers can choose to purchase a domain from other providers such as GoDaddy.

A custom domain can significantly improve the visibility and professionalism of your Etsy shop. It also makes it easier to point people to your shop rather than giving them the long Etsy URL version. And even if you don't think you need a dedicated URL, it's a good idea to lock one in so someone else doesn't claim it.

Featured Items: Featured items are listings or shop sections that are prominently displayed on a seller's shop page. All sellers on Etsy have the **standard grid** option, which allows you to feature up to four listings or shop sections on your shop's page.

Etsy Plus subscribers have the additional option to use a **mixed grid layout.** With a mixed grid layout, *Etsy Plus* subscribers can feature one big listing or shop section along with four smaller items or shop sections on their shop page.

While you do not have to feature any items at the top of your store, if you do, be sure to carefully select the items or sections you want to feature as they will be prominently displayed to customers and could impact their buying decisions. For example, if you selected Christmas items to be highlighted during the holiday season, don't forget to change them out after December 25th. Leaving up outdated featured items may make customers question how committed you are to your shop.

Should you start your Etsy digital download shop with *Etsy Standard* or upgrade to *Etsy Plus*? That is a choice only you can make. Most sellers start with *Etsy Standard* and then upgrade to *Etsy Plus* as their business grows. The listing and ad credits, the customization options, the advanced shop management, and promotional tools, and the priority customer support are, in my opinion, all well worth the $10 monthly fee. And since you pay on a month-to-month basis, you can cancel your subscription at any time and revert to *Etsy Standard.*

Etsy Shop Icon: Your Etsy shop icon, also known as your logo or profile picture, is a small image that serves as the visual representation of your shop on the Etsy platform. It appears alongside your shop name on your shop's homepage, on your listings, and on various other pages on the Etsy website and app. Your shop icon is a crucial component of your branding and should ideally be used across all your social media platforms to maintain consistency and brand recognition. This means that your Etsy shop icon should be the same profile picture on every website where your business has a presence.

To set up your **Etsy shop icon**, you will need to follow these steps:

1. Sign into your Etsy account and go to the **Shop Manager** section.
2. Click on **Settings** and then click on the **Info & Appearance** tab.
3. Scroll down to the **Shop Icon** section and click on the **Change Icon** button.
4. Select the image you want to use as your shop icon from your computer or device. The image must be at least 500 x 500 pixels and in a .jpg, .gif, or .png format.
5. Click on the **Save** button to apply your changes.

Shop Story: An **Etsy shop story** is where you can share a summary of your shop's products, your overall brand, your business goals, and a bit about you as a person. Connecting with shoppers in this way shows them you are a real person, which can go a long way toward building trust and confidence with your buyers.

To set up your **Etsy shop story** follow these steps:

1. Sign into your Etsy account and click on the **Shop Manager** button in the top right corner of the page.
2. Click on the **Settings** tab and then click on the **About Your Shop** tab.
3. Click on the **Story tab** at the top of the page.
4. Enter in a **Story Headline.**
5. Fill in the **Story** field.
6. You can also add a **Shop Video** here.
7. You can also add in **Shop Photos.**
8. You can also **add links to your social media pages**.
9. Click on the **Save** button to apply your changes.

Etsy Shop Title & Shop Announcement: The *Shop Title* and *Shop Announcement* are important parts of your Etsy shop's storefront as they appear at the top of your shop's homepage, meaning they are the first sections customers will see when visiting your shop.

Your *Shop Title* should be a short and catchy phrase that represents your store and the products you offer. On the other hand, your

Shop Announcement is a brief message that can be used to share important time-sensitive information with your customers, such as new product launches, promotions, or updated policies.

To create a *Shop Title,* choose a phrase that accurately reflects your shop's products and style. For the *Shop Announcement*, craft a message that is informative and engaging, and consider adding relevant keywords to maximize your Etsy SEO.

To access your *Shop Title* and *Shop Announcement* sections, click on the **Settings** tab in your **Shop Manager** and then click on **Info & Appearance.** You can change these areas at any time or leave them blank until you have built up your shop and are more comfortable filling them out.

Message to Buyers: Also under the Info & Appearance section is a space to write a message to your buyers that Etsy will automatically include on receipt pages and in the email they send to buyers whenever they place an order on the site. A simple "thank you for your order" message with a general statement about shipping is enough to include here, although this is an optional field.

Message to Buyers for Digital Items: Also under the Info & Appearance section is a space to write a message to buyers for digital items. Etsy offers the following directions for this section: If you sell digital items, we will include this message on the

Downloads page for digital orders. It applies to all digital listings purchased from your shop.

It is in this section that you can provide a general message to your buyers. Note that this is an optional field. If you are offering different files or selling some items that can be customized, it might confuse buyers to have a message from you here. If you are selling as-is items that are only available in one type of file, say coloring pages in PDF format, you could include the instructions for how to download the files you sell.

Etsy Shop Banner: An Etsy shop banner is a large image that appears at the top of your shop's homepage and gives potential customers an idea of what your shop is all about. Just as with your *Shop Title* and *Shop Announcement*, your banner image is an important element of your shop's appearance, as it helps create a professional and cohesive look for your shop. And while you don't have to have a shop banner, it's an easy way to contribute to the branding of your business.

To edit your Etsy Banner, first, log into your **Shop Manager**. Then **click on the pencil icon next to your shop's name**. This will bring up a page where you can edit your shop's banner.

Just as you want your Etsy shop icon to be cohesive across all of your social media platforms, you want to do the same with your banner. Facebook and YouTube both allow banners, and it's easy to place your Etsy banner on both of those sites.

Mixed Grid: All Etsy shops have the option to use a *Standard Grid* but *Etsy Plus* shops can also choose a *Mixed Grid* option that features five listings or shop sections with a couple of layout choices.

To edit your grid options, first, log into your **Shop Manager**. Then **click on the pencil icon next to your shop's name**. This will bring up a page where you can edit your shop's **Featured Items** with your grid options. Some sellers change their grid options every day to ensure returning customers are always greeted with a new look. However, most sellers opt to change them once a week or once a month.

Hiring Out Design Services: When building your Etsy business, you want to use consistent shop graphics across all of your social media platforms to create a cohesive brand image. If you aren't able to design your logos and banners yourself, or you simply don't have the time to create them, you can hire graphic designers.

There are several places where you can hire a designer to create your Etsy shop logo, icons, and banners. Some options include:

1. **Fiverr:** Fiverr is an online marketplace where you can find freelance designers who offer a wide range of design services, including logo and banner design. You can browse

through portfolios and reviews to find a designer who meets your needs and budget. It's easy to find a designer for under $10, especially new designers on the site who are eager to build their portfolios. I recommend choosing designers that offer at least two revisions of your order to ensure you get exactly what you want.

2. **Upwork:** Upwork is another online marketplace where you can find freelance designers for hire. You can post a job listing and receive proposals from designers who are interested in working with you. You will likely pay more for a designer on UpWork versus Fiverr, but the quality may also be better. Just like new designers on Fiverr charge less, you may find new designers on UpWork who are willing to do the job for less money to build their portfolio. As with Fiverr, I recommend choosing designers that offer at least two revisions.

3. **99designs:** 99designs is a design contest platform where you can hold a design contest to receive multiple design options for your logo, icons, and banners. You can choose the design you like best and work with the designer to make any necessary revisions.

4. **Etsy:** You can also find designers on Etsy who offer design services, including logo and banner design.

Shop Options: You can find **Options** under the **Settings** tab in your shop managers. Etsy allows you to pre-determine several options for your store, including:

- **Rearrange Your Shop:** You can enable the feature to allow shop visitors to sort listings to their specifications. Or you can disable this feature so that the *Most Recently Listed* option is chosen. Some sellers opt to have their best-selling products listed first. Or they are constantly rearranging the listings so that their shop always looks fresh.

- **Custom Order Requests:** If you are offering custom or personalized digital products, you can enable a setting where a *Request Custom Order* button will appear across your shop. If you do not offer personalized items, you will want to disable this feature so customers know that the products you are selling are as pictured.

- **Offer Gift Wrapping & Gift Message:** Since you are selling digital products, you will want to disable these options.

- **Sold Listings:** You can choose to let other Etsy users see your sold listings, or you can hide them. Some sellers choose to hide their sold listings for fear that other sellers will see and then steal their best-selling designs. I let users see my sold listings so that customers can see my most popular items, which might help them decide to purchase them, too.

- **Current Time Zone:** You can set your shop's time zone here. This is helpful when you are shipping physical products as it lets customers know where you are located in relation to them so that they will have a better idea of how long shipping may take. However, with digital products, this isn't necessary information unless you offer customization. Then it might make sense to list your time zone so that customers will have a better understanding of your working hours.

- **Vacation Mode:** If you ever need to put your Etsy shop on vacation (whether because you are taking an actual vacation or are simply unable to process orders), you can easily put your entire store on vacation so that customers cannot purchase anything from your store. In fact, while your storefront will still be visible, your listings will be hidden. You can also include a *Vacation Announcement* that will display at the top of your shop. And you can write up a *Messages Autoreply*, which will be sent to anyone who sends you a message while your *Vacation Mode* is on. It's good to know how to quickly put your shop on vacation in case of an emergency and to make sure someone close to you knows how to, as well.

- **Close Shop:** Also under the *Options* section is a tab to close your Etsy shop. Note that if you have *Etsy Standard,* you only pay when you list an item. So, there is no reason to close your shop if you simply aren't listing new products. If you have an *Etsy Plus* account, you can simply cancel that subscription and leave your shop as is, even if there are no listings.

Shipping Policies: The shipping settings section of your Etsy account (accessible under the **Settings** tab) is where you can manage and configure the shipping options for your shop. Note that you can create shipping profiles within each of your listings to match up with the various products you are selling.

The biggest advantage of selling digital products is that there is no shipping involved. You upload your files to Etsy, and when a customer purchases one, Etsy facilitates the digital delivery of your file.

Policy Settings: Also under the Settings section is where you can create your Policy Settings. Here you can set up the following:

- **Returns & Exchanges:** Etsy allows sellers to set their own policies for returns and exchanges on their products. The good news is that Etsy doesn't allow returns of digital products as once the customer downloads a file, they can't remove it from their system and send it back. All sales are final unless the seller made an error with the product. For example, if you sell custom items and make a mistake when personalizing the product. In that case, you would need to make a new file and send it to the customer.

- **Cancellations:** The cancellations setting on Etsy allows sellers to set their policies for canceling orders. These policies can vary from seller to seller and can include information on the conditions under which a buyer can cancel an order and any fees that may be associated with the cancellation. With a digital product that is being sold as-is (i.e. not customized), the transfer of the product happens immediately after a buyer purchases, meaning they won't be able to cancel as it falls under Etsy's policy of not allowing returns of digital products. If a customer asks to cancel a custom order before you have started working on it, it's considered good customer service to go ahead and cancel it. Make sure your policies give a clear timeline as to how long a customer has to cancel custom orders. You don't want to accept cancellations of products you've already worked to customize.

- **Privacy:** The privacy settings on Etsy allow users to control how their personal information is collected, used, and shared on the platform. These settings include options for controlling the types of information that is shared with Etsy and third-party partners, as well as options for managing communication preferences and account settings. In the privacy settings, users can choose to limit the types of information that Etsy collects from them, such as browsing data or search queries.

- **Fixed Polices**: The fixed policies section in an Etsy seller's dashboard is a set of pre-written templates that sellers can use to quickly create their shop policies, such as their shipping, returns, and payment policies. These templates provide a basic framework for the seller to follow but can be customized to suit the specific needs of the seller and their business. Again, unless you are selling custom products, digital items are sold as-is with Etsy immediately transferring the file to the buyer and no returns are allowed.

Production Partners: Unless you are creating your digital products completely on your own, you will always have at least one *Production Partner* for all of your Etsy listings.

I have several *Production Partners* entered for my shop. Not only do I have them in the main *Production Partners* section, but I then choose which ones are specific for each listing. For example, if I purchased a graphic on Creative Fabrica and then added that graphic to a page I bought from Tangent Template that I edited using Canva, I would select all three of those companies as the *Production Partners* when I listed that product.

Not adding *Production Partners* can mean a designer could file a trademark infringement complaint on your listing, even if you purchased the graphic legally. Unfortunately, many Etsy shops steal artwork and try to pass it off as their own, meaning artists and designers have to keep their eyes on the site to see if someone is selling their work.

PRO TIP: When I first started selling digital products, I didn't realize I needed to enter *Production Partners* and a designer filed a copyright claim against me, which caused Etsy to remove my listings. Even though I had purchased the graphics legally, I hadn't entered *Production Partners,* so the original designer genuinely believed I had stolen their work. Keeping up with entering any *Production Partners* you use is necessary to protect your business.

Community & Help: You can keep up with all of Etsy's announcements as well as get help under the *Community & Help* section, which is linked in your Shop Manager. You can also access the *Help Center* from any Etsy page directly on the site by scrolling down to the very bottom and locating the *Help* section.

Facebook Shops: *Facebook Shops* is a feature on the Etsy seller dashboard that enables you to connect your Etsy shop with your Facebook account and establish a store on Facebook. This will allow you to sell your products directly on Facebook, in addition to your Etsy shop.

When you connect your Etsy shop to Facebook, you can easily transfer your products, product information, and inventory to your Facebook store. Furthermore, once connected, you can sync your inventory and sales across both platforms, so you don't have to worry about managing stock levels or order fulfillment between the two.

It is important to note that you will need to have a Facebook page set up before creating a store and linking it to your Etsy shop. We will discuss creating a Facebook page for your business later in this book. Additionally, Facebook has certain policies and guidelines regarding the use of its platform for commerce, so make sure to familiarize yourself with them before utilizing *Facebook Shops.*

Etsy Fees: Now that you have your shop set up, let's go over the fees that Etsy charges for listing items for sale on their site:

Listing Fees: Etsy charges a $.20 fee to list an item for four months. This $.20 fee is charged whenever you create a new listing or relist an expired one. Note that this fee is for one LISTING. You may list several items within one listing if you have different variations of it. For example, in my Etsy sticker shop, I sell matte stickers, holographic stickers, and magnets of the same design. I create one listing for each design but offer all three options under each listing. I don't pay for each variation. I only pay the $.20 fee for the single listing.

While no one likes to pay fees, the $.20 listing fee on Etsy is quite low, especially when compared to other e-commerce sites like Amazon or eBay. At the end of the four months, you can opt to renew the listing for another four months at the same cost of $0.20, making the total cost for one item to be listed for a full year only $0.80.

Transaction Fees: In addition to the listing fee, Etsy also charges a transaction fee on each sale that you make. Like their low listing fees, this 5% transaction fee on Etsy is a small price to pay for the exposure and resources provided by the platform, including payment processing and file delivery. The fee is calculated on the sale price of each item, including shipping and gift-wrapping charges if there are any, and it helps cover the costs of running and maintaining the Etsy website.

Payment Processing Fees: Etsy makes it easy for customers to pay using a variety of methods as it partners with different payment processors to handle transactions, and these processors charge various fees for their services. This fee is typically around 2.9% + $.30 per transaction, which allows customers to pay for their orders using their debit cards, credit cards, or even PayPal. If you had to arrange payment processing yourself, it would cost much more. Not only does Etsy handle the payments from buyers, but they also handle the distribution of your profits to your bank account.

Advertising & Promotional Fees: In addition to the fees outlined above, Etsy offers various advertising and promotional options for sellers who want to increase the visibility of their products. These options come with additional fees, which vary depending on the specific advertising or promotion being used.

Etsy Ads: Just listing products for sale on Etsy may not be enough to get customers to find your items. That's where *Etsy Ads* come in. *Etsy Ads* is an advertising program that lets you promote your products right on the Etsy site.

To get started with *Etsy Ads,* just head to your **Seller Dashboard**, click on the **Marketing** tab, and select **Etsy Ads**. Keep in mind that you have to pay every time someone clicks on your ad, regardless of whether or not they make a purchase. If you want to test Etsy ads, I recommend starting with a $5 daily budget for a month to see how your ads perform. You can adjust your budget at any time to fit your needs or you can cancel the ad if you aren't seeing results.

Etsy Offsite Ads: Unlike regular *Etsy Ads*, which are only shown on Etsy and for which you have to pay every time someone clicks on your ad, *Etsy Offsite Ads* offer sellers a chance to expand their reach beyond the Etsy marketplace and potentially increase sales by showcasing their products to shoppers on Google and other search engine sites. To enable this feature, go to your *Seller Dashboard*, click on the *Settings* tab, and select *Offsite Ads*.

If you sell less than $10,000 in a year on Etsy, you can choose whether or not to participate in *Etsy Offsite Ads*. However, if you exceed $10,000 in annual sales, *Offsite Ads* become mandatory.

While some sellers don't like the idea of mandatory participation, remember that you only pay for an ad when someone clicks on it AND then makes a purchase from your shop. Since you only pay for the ad when someone orders something from you, there is no risk to the program.

PRO TIP: Because I focus heavily on Etsy SEO, I don't run regular *Etsy Ads*. However, I do make sure I have opted into the *Offsite Ads* program. Again, I only pay for an offsite advertisement when it leads to a sale. To me, *Offsite Ads* are essentially free advertising for me as they bring people to my shop. If they make a purchase, I am then charged a small fee, which is easily covered by the money I made with the sale. Running my own Google Ads would cost a fortune, so the *Etsy Offsite Ads* program is a great benefit for me.

Payment Processing: When I started selling online in 2005 on eBay, getting paid was sometimes quite a challenge. Back then, PayPal was the primary payment system used by eBay, and some customers were hesitant to trust the site. So some buyers sent me checks and even cash and checks through the mail to pay for their orders!

Fortunately, payment processing is now integrated into all online selling platforms, including Etsy. Thanks to *Etsy Payments*, I don't have to worry about collecting payments from my customers. Buyers can pay for their orders using different methods, such as credit and debit cards, PayPal, and gift cards. Etsy handles the payment processing, holding the funds in escrow until the seller confirms the shipment of the order. This means that there's no need for sellers to send invoices or chase down payments, as everything is automated through Etsy.

When you sell digital products, the payment processes immediately. Etsy does not transfer your digital file to the customer until their payment clears. If there is an issue with a customer's payment, Etsy handles it. You as the seller will never even know there was an issue as the sale won't be complete until the buyer's payment is processed.

To use *Etsy Payments,* sellers must enroll in the service and link a bank account to their Etsy account to receive payouts from Etsy. When an order is placed in your shop, Etsy automatically processes the payment from the customer. The total amount is deducted for fees and shipping costs, and the remaining funds are deposited into your Etsy account. You can then choose to have these funds transferred to your bank account on a schedule you choose (daily, weekly, bi-weekly, or monthly). I like weekly payouts as it gives me a regular paycheck to look forward to.

Sales Tax: Selling on Etsy comes with a key advantage of the platform handling state sales tax collection and remittance on behalf of its sellers. This saves sellers a significant amount of time and effort as we don't have to collect and remit sales tax individually to each state, a requirement in most American states for online orders. This benefit of selling on Etsy is a major factor in why many sellers opt to keep their shop on the platform instead of setting up their own Shopify store. In fact, I have met successful Etsy shop owners who expanded to Shopify only to eventually go back to selling exclusively on Etsy for the sales tax collection alone!

Seller Protection: Etsy provides several protections for sellers on its platform, including:

Payment Protection: With Etsy Payments, buyers' funds are securely held until the order has been completed and the package has been delivered. If you are selling digital products as-is, the payment will process immediately. If you are selling custom digital products, the payment will process once you deliver the completed file to your buyer.

Dispute Resolution: Etsy's dispute resolution process is designed to help sellers and buyers resolve issues in a fair and timely manner. The process can involve either mediation, where Etsy acts as a mediator to facilitate communication between the parties, or arbitration, where Etsy makes a final decision on the dispute.

Both sellers and buyers can get help resolving any disputes through **Etsy's Help section.** Simply **scroll down to the bottom of any Etsy page** and locate the **Help** heading. Underneath, click on **Help Center.**

When possible, do your best to resolve customer issues on your own. With digital products, if the error is yours, you need to make it right as quickly as possible. However, if a customer simply has buyer's remorse, be kind but firm in your response. Unlike selling physical products that might break or get lost in the mail, the main issue with digital products is usually that a customer is confused about how to download the files they purchased. Having an automated response with instructions about how to download and open the files you sell will save you time and frustration. I keep instructions on downloading files in a Word document that I can easily copy and paste into my replies to buyers.

Seller Protection Insurance: Etsy offers seller protection insurance to eligible sellers in certain countries for orders under $250. While Etsy does not allow returns or exchanges on digital products, they may refund buyers and allow sellers to keep their earnings if a buyer claims the file was lost or damaged or if they claim an item doesn't match the listing even though photos prove it does. This protection is more for sellers who sell physical items such as crafts and antiques.

PRO TIP: If a buyer contacts you claiming an item hasn't been delivered but tracking shows it has, direct them to file a claim directly through Etsy. They can do this by clicking directly on their order and following the prompts on the screen. This removes you from the dispute process and puts the burden on Etsy directly to resolve the issue.

Shop Sections: When it comes to organizing your Etsy shop, *Shop Sections* are your friend! These handy sections (also known as store categories) allow you to group your products into easy-to-navigate categories. This makes it simple for customers to find what they're looking for and for you to manage your inventory and listings more effectively.

As a digital product seller, you can use *Shop Sections* to group your products by design, theme, product type, or whatever works best for you. This makes it easy for customers to find products in the niche they are shopping for. And on the back end, *Shop Sections* are a great way for you as a seller to keep things organized.

To set up your Shop Sections, go to your **Seller Dashboard** and click on the **Listings** tab. On the right-hand side of the page will be the heading **Sections** with a drop-down menu underneath. Click on **Manage** to add and rearrange your shop categories. I personally like to arrange mine in alphabetical order.

Creating sections based on your different categories, niches, or special occasions and holidays will help customers easily narrow down the search results in your store. For example, if you plan to sell digital planners and have sets targeted to various professions, you could create sections based on the different careers. Maybe you create sections for teachers, nurses, lawyers, stay-at-home parents, etc. On the other hand, if you have coloring book pages for various holidays, you can create sections for Christmas, Valentine's Day, Easter, etc.

When an Etsy shopper is looking at one item in your shop, Etsy will show them products you offer based on your *Shop Sections.* If a buyer is looking at a listing for your Christmas coloring pages, Etsy will show them the other items listed in that same section. If they show the customer your other Christmas coloring pages, that buyer may end up purchasing two or more sets from you.

PRO TIP: One key aspect of Etsy is its search engine optimization or SEO. When you list an item, make sure to use the same keywords in the title, description, and tags. Additionally, aligning your shop sections with these categories can also help with SEO. For example, if you sell digital budget trackers, make sure "digital budget tracker" is included in the title, description, tags, and store category section.

CHAPTER FIVE: LISTING DIGITAL PRODUCTS ON ETSY

The exciting part of your journey is finally here: It's time to start listing your digital products on Etsy and earning money! After all the research and hard work you've put in to create these items, it's time to get them out there for customers to buy. As we've discussed earlier, there are two main types of digital products: those that you sell as-is and those that you personalize for your customers.

Let's start with listing products that you are selling as-is, such as planner pages, coloring books, workbooks, trackers, and such. This means that the customer will be purchasing exactly what is pictured in the listing. You will not be offering any customization or personalization options for these items.

For this example, let's say you have created a PDF file of 10 children's coloring book pages. Here are the steps you need to take to list this file:

Log in to your Etsy account and click on the **Shop Manager** button on the top right-hand corner of the screen. Click on the **Listings** tab and then click on the **Add a listing** button.

PHOTOS

Photos: The first field you will need to fill in is photos of your products. When it comes to creating photos for your digital products on Etsy, there are a few approaches you can take:

1. **Create digital mockups:** One way to showcase your digital products is to create digital mockups. For example, if you're selling a PDF of a coloring book, you could create mockups that show the book's cover or a few sample pages in use. You can use graphic design tools like Canva or Photoshop to create these mockups, or you can use a mockup generator tool like Placeit.

2. **Use product images:** Another approach is to use product images that show your digital product in use. For example, you could print out your coloring pages and place them with some crayons to show that they are meant for children.

3. **Create illustrations:** Note that if you're selling digital products like clip art or digital paper, you can create illustrations or graphics to showcase them. This can help give customers an idea of what they can create with your product and how it can be used.

Remember, the goal of your product photos is to showcase your digital product in the best way possible and give customers a clear idea of what they are purchasing. Whatever approach you take, make sure the photos are high-quality, well-lit, and accurately represent your product.

When it comes to creating photos for digital products, I like to keep things simple and use Canva Pro. It's quick and easy to upload my PDF files to Canva and create a **2000x2000 pixels image frame**, which is the best size for Etsy photos. If I'm selling a single-page product, I just put that one page in the frame. If there is white space around it, I might choose a color for the background to help make the image pop.

For products with multiple pages, like our children's coloring book example, I select a few pages to showcase in the thumbnail photo. I will then create some single-page frames to add to the listing. Once I'm happy with the images, I download them to my computer and then upload them directly to my Etsy listing.

Adjust Thumbnail: When you upload a photo to Etsy, it will automatically generate a thumbnail photo that will appear as the main image in your listing. This thumbnail photo needs to be 2000x2000 pixels. However, the actual photo you upload can be larger than 2000x2000 pixels, but it will be automatically resized to fit the requirements. If your photo is not 2000x2000 pixels or larger, Etsy may not accept it and you will need to adjust the size before uploading it.

To adjust the thumbnail photo, you can edit the listing and click on the thumbnail photo to select a different area of the image to use as the thumbnail. This may be necessary if the automatic cropping does not show the desired portion of the photo.

Video: Etsy now allows sellers to add videos to their listings, which is great news for sellers of digital products who want to showcase items more dynamically. Using our coloring book example, you could add a video of you flipping through the pages to give customers a better idea of what they're getting. Or you might use a colored pencil or crayon to color in a small section.

Using a smartphone is a quick and easy way to create a video that showcases your digital product. All you need is a steady hand and good lighting. Etsy videos have no sound, so you don't have to worry about talking or using music. Note that you can only add one video to each listing. And all videos are limited to only 15 seconds.

To create a video for your Etsy listing, simply use your phone's camera to record a short clip of your digital product. Using the example of the children's coloring book digital download, you could film a short clip of a child coloring on one of the pages or flipping through the book. Be creative and think about what would be visually appealing to potential customers.

PRO TIP: Product videos can be time-consuming to create and upload, especially if you are trying to add videos to every single listing. Ask yourself if the product you are selling needs a video for it to sell. If the answer is 'no', spend your time on the other sections of your Etsy listing that are more important.

Etsy SEO: Before we tackle the remaining fields in an Etsy listing, we first need to talk about Etsy SEO, which is *Search Engine Optimization*. While it may sound intimidating, it just means using the right keywords to help your products show up in search results when customers are looking for something specific. This is key to getting your products seen and, ultimately, making sales.

There are several places in your Etsy listing where you can use keywords to optimize your SEO, including the title, description, tags, and even your shop's sections. The title is one of the most important places to include keywords because it is what customers see first in search results. It's important to make sure your title accurately reflects your product and includes relevant keywords that customers might use to search for it.

The description is another key place to use keywords. This is where you can provide more information about your product and its features, as well as include additional keywords that might not fit in the title. However, it's important to keep your description clear and concise, so customers can easily understand what you're selling. Some sellers make the mistake of simply typing hundreds of keywords into their descriptions rather than writing a readable description that not only tells the customer exactly what the product is but also 'sells' it to them by touting its benefits over other products on the site.

Tags are another way to optimize your SEO. These are keywords that you can add to your listing to help customers find it when they search for something specific. You can add up to 13 tags per listing, so make sure to choose ones that accurately describe your product and are relevant to your target audience.

Lastly, your shop's sections can also be optimized for SEO. By using keywords in your sections that you also used in your titles, descriptions, and tags, you are telling Etsy that these are the most important keywords for your product, which will help Etsy match your listings to buyers searching with those keywords.

Optimizing your Etsy SEO is a crucial part of selling on the platform. By using the right keywords in strategic places throughout your listing and shop, you can increase visibility and ultimately drive more sales. While it may seem tedious to repeat your keywords in several places, it is a critical part of selling on Etsy. Therefore, you need to keep SEO in mind every time you create a new Etsy listing.

LISTING DETAILS

Title: The title section of an Etsy listing is one of the most important elements of your product listing. It's the first thing potential buyers will see when they search for products on Etsy, so you want to make sure it's clear, descriptive, and engaging. When creating a title for your listing, think about the keywords and phrases that your target audience is likely to search for. Make sure your title accurately reflects the product you are selling and includes important details, such as the product type, materials, size, and any unique features.

Using our example of a digital download of a 10-page children's coloring book, a good title might be "10-Page Children's Coloring Book Digital Download, Printable PDF, Instant Download, Printable Coloring Pages, Kids Activity Book". This title includes important details such as the number of pages, product type (digital download), and key features (printable, instant download).

Remember that Etsy's search algorithm considers the keywords used in your title, so be sure to include relevant keywords to help your listing appear in search results. However, it's essential to avoid "keyword stuffing" or using irrelevant keywords just to attract more views. This can harm your ranking in search results and potentially result in account suspension.

About this listing: Etsy allows you to sell three types of products: handmade items, vintage items, and craft supplies. The *About This Listing* section requires you to specify what category your product falls under. Digital products are typically listed under handmade. There are three sections under *About This Listing*:

- **Who Made It? Select a Maker:** Choose from *I Did, A Member of My Shop*, or *Another Company or Shop*. For digital products, you will select *I Did*. Even if you purchased templates and graphics from another source, since you created the digital file, it is technically handmade by you.
- **What Is It? Select a Use:** Choose from *A Finished Product* or *A Supply or Tool To Make Things*. For digital products, you will select *A Finished Product*. Even if you are selling customized products, your PDF is a product in and of itself.
- **When Was It Made?:** Choose from *Made To Order, Recently*, or *Vintage*. If you are selling digital products that you will customize, select *Made To Order*. Otherwise, choose a date range under *Recently*. I choose the year I first created the download.

Note that if you offer personalization, you need to select *Made To Order*.

Category: Select the **Category** that best fits your product. When you are listing anything on Etsy, I recommend using the *Category* search feature to see what options Etsy gives you. Sometimes they will pre-offer you options based on your title. For our example of a coloring book, Etsy would show you several category options, including a category for *Coloring Books*.

Colors: Depending on the category you list your item in, Etsy may offer you the ability to choose a primary and secondary color for your item. Both of these are optional fields.

Occasion: Depending on the category you list your item in, Etsy may offer you the ability to choose an occasion for your item. Occasions include events such as birthdays, weddings, anniversaries, retirements, baby showers, and graduations. This field is optional.

Holiday: Depending on the category you list your item in, Etsy may offer you the ability to choose a holiday for your item. Holidays are events such as Christmas, Valentine's Day, Easter, Mother's Day, Father's Day, Halloween, and Thanksgiving. This field is optional.

Theme: Depending on the category you list your item in, Etsy may offer you the ability to choose a theme for your product. Themes may include things such as Animals, Beach & Tropical, Bugs & Insects, Fantasy & Sci-Fi, Floral, Food & Drink, Letters & Words, Love & Friendship, and more. Choosing a theme is optional.

Renewal options: When you create a new listing on Etsy, you can choose how long the listing will be active. By default, listings are set to be active for a minimum of four months. After four months, the listing will expire, and you will need to renew it to continue selling the item.

When you renew a listing, it becomes active again, and it will appear in search results and your shop's listings. Renewing a listing also resets its place in the search results, giving it a higher chance of being seen by potential buyers.

There are two ways to renew a listing: manually or automatically. Manually renewing a listing means that your listings will end after four months, and you will then go in and renew each expired listing individually. You can do this by logging into your seller dashboard and going to the *Listing Status* field on the right-hand side of the page. Underneath you will see if you have any *Expired, Sold Out,* or *Inactive* listings. Listings that have automatically ended after four months will be located under *Expired.* You will be charged $0.20 each time a listing renews, either manually or automatically.

Automatic renewal, on the other hand, means that Etsy will automatically renew your expired listings for you. You can set up automatic renewal for individual listings or all of your listings. When a listing is automatically renewed, Etsy charges you the $0.20 listing fee, and the renewed listing will be active for another four months.

To keep things simple, I suggest selecting to manually renew all new listings. After four months, the listing will expire. If the product has been selling well, you can renew the listing as-is and change it to automatically renew. But if it hasn't sold in those first four months, you may want to edit the listing by changing the photos or adding new keywords to the title, description, and tags before manually renewing it for another four months. If the product still hasn't sold after another four months, you might try one more four-month period before deciding if you want to keep renewing the listing or deleting it altogether to focus on products that are selling.

Type: Etsy allows sellers to offer either **Physical** or **Digital** products. This one is easy: you select *Digital*!

Description: The description field in an Etsy listing is where you can give more detailed information about your digital product. It's an opportunity to describe the content of your product, the size, and any other pertinent information you think the customer should know. Even though you may include some of this information in other sections of the listing, it's important to repeat all pertinent information in the description.

Most online sellers will tell you that online shoppers are notorious for not reading listings thoroughly before they order; but ensuring you fill out every part of the listing, including the description, will protect you if a buyer wants to return an item for a reason you listed simply because they didn't read the description.

As I've mentioned several times now, to maximize Etsy SEO, it's important to use keywords from your title and in your description. For example, when listing our 10-page children's coloring book as a digital download, in the description field, you would want to include the same keywords you used in the listing title. However, you don't want to just copy and paste your title into the description but rather work the keywords into natural sentences. A good description could be:

Looking for a fun and engaging activity for your child? Look no further than our 10-page children's coloring book! This digital download features printable 8.5" by 11" PDF pages that are perfect for keeping little ones entertained and creative. With instant download, you can have these printable coloring pages in your hands in no time. Our kid's activity book is filled with whimsical illustrations and designs that are sure to spark your child's imagination. Plus, with the convenience of being able to print the pages at home, you can easily stock up on a variety of coloring books to keep on hand for rainy days, car trips, and more. So what are you waiting for? Add our 10-page children's coloring book digital download to your collection today and give your child the gift of artistic expression and fun!

Production Partners: The *Production Partners* section is a section within an Etsy listing where a seller can indicate if someone other than themselves (i.e., a production partner) is involved in the creation or manufacturing of the item being sold. If you are purchasing templates or graphics to use in your digital products, you must enter the companies you bought those design elements from in this section. Failure to do so can result in the original designer filing a trademark infringement case against you through Etsy, or worse, suing you directly.

For my Etsy business, I have several different *Production Partners*. I have all of them linked in my account, and for each listing, I select the ones that I used for that particular product. Using the coloring book example, let's say I purchased the coloring book pages on Creative Fabrica and edited them in Canva using some of the elements within Canva Pro to add to the pages. For this listing, I would make sure that Creative Fabrica and Canva are selected as production partners. And don't worry about your customer seeing the names of your *Production Partners* as you can make them private. All your buyers will see is that you utilized *Production Partners* in the creation of your products.

Section: One of the great features of having an Etsy shop is the ability to create *Sections*, also referred to as *Categories*, for your listings. You can have up to 20 *Sections*, and you can arrange them in any way you want. I usually choose to sort mine alphabetically.

Remember that to maximize Etsy SEO you want important keywords to be repeated in the *Title, Description, Tags*, and *Sections*. For the coloring book example, I would make a section for *Children's Coloring Books*. I would then make sure that *Children's Coloring Books* was in the listing title, description, and tags.

You can edit, add, or delete your shop *Sections* at any time as well as rearrange them in whatever order you prefer.

Tags: Tags are an important part of maximizing your Etsy SEO, as they help buyers find your items through Etsy's search function. Essentially, tags are keywords that you assign to your listing, and when a buyer searches for those keywords, your item will appear in the search results. Here's how tags work in an Etsy listing:

1. You can add up to 13 tags per listing. When you're creating or editing a listing, you'll see a field where you can enter your tags.

2. Think about the keywords that a buyer might use to search for your item. For example, if you're selling digital planners, you might use tags like "planners," "digital planners," "planner downloads," and "planner printables."

3. Don't use irrelevant tags. Using tags that have nothing to do with your item might attract more views, but they won't be helpful to buyers who are looking for something specific. And it may anger potential customers.

4. If a product isn't selling, try using different tags. It's a good idea to review and update your tags periodically to make sure they are still relevant and effective.

Finding the appropriate tags can sometimes be a struggle. I use both eRank.com and EtsyCheck.com to search for the best keywords for each of my listings. I simply type in the name of what I am listing, and both programs generate a list of potential tags. For the children's coloring book digital download, EtsyCheck.com gave me the following options:

- Digital download
- Coloring book
- Coloring pages
- Children
- Instant download
- Printable
- Colouring book
- Printable coloring
- Coloring
- Kids
- Download
- Digital
- PDF
- Coloring page
- Childrens coloring
- Activity book
- Fun
- Book
- Coloring sheets
- Digital coloring
- Art

- Kids coloring book
- Kids colouring book
- Print

There are clearly more than 13 *Tags* for me to choose from, meaning I will have to narrow down my choices. The keywords are ranked from most searched to least searched, but I like to choose a variety. The most searched *Tags* also have the most competition. Therefore, choosing half that are the most used with half that aren't gives me a better chance of reaching the most customers.

As we've already discussed, to maximize Etsy SEO, you want to make sure the same keywords in your *Title, Description*, and shop *Sections* are replicated in your *Tags*. This use of SEO is what sets the top Etsy shops apart from the competition. So while it may seem tedious, it is worth your time to get it right.

Materials: The *Materials* section of an Etsy listing is an optional field located directly underneath the *Tags* section where the seller can list the physical materials used to make the item being sold. This section is typically used for physical products such as handmade items, supplies, and vintage goods. However, for digital downloads, you can still fill out the *Materials* section to provide information about what software or tools are required to use the digital files.

Here are some tips for filling out the *Materials* section for digital downloads:

1. List the software or tools required to use the digital files. For example, if you're selling a set of Photoshop brushes, you could list "Adobe Photoshop" as the material.
2. Be specific and accurate. You don't want to list anything that doesn't relate to your product as it will confuse customers.
3. Use common terms that buyers will understand. For instance, instead of listing "EPS," which may be unfamiliar to some buyers, use "vector file" instead.
4. if your digital download includes multiple file formats, list them all in the *Materials* section.
5. If your digital download doesn't require any specific materials, you can simply state "digital file" in the *Materials* section.

Remember, while the *Materials* section is optional and may not be as relevant for digital downloads as it is for physical products, it's still worth considering filling out. The *Materials* can also act as additional keywords in Etsy's search algorithm. EtsyCheck.com, which I use to generate tags, also generates appropriate *Materials* for me to add to my listings.

INVENTORY AND PRICING

Price: You likely want to start selling digital downloads to make money, and we're finally at the section of your listing for you to price your items. But how do you know what to charge for your digital products? When it comes to pricing digital products, there are several things to consider:

1. **Time and effort:** Consider the time and effort that went into creating the digital product. Consider any research, design, or development that was necessary to create the product.

2. **Value to the buyer:** Think about the value that the digital product provides to the buyer. Will it help them save time, make money, or solve a problem? Consider the benefits that the buyer will receive from the product and how that impacts its value.

3. **Competition:** Research what similar digital products are being sold on Etsy and other marketplaces. This can give you an idea of the going rate for similar products and help you price your own accordingly.

4. **Costs:** While digital products don't require physical materials or shipping, there may still be costs associated with creating and selling them. Consider any software, equipment, or website fees that you incurred during the creation or sale of the product.

When pricing your digital products on Etsy, you'll also need to consider the platform's fees. Remember that Etsy charges a $0.20

listing fee and a 5% transaction fee on the sale price (including shipping). Be sure to factor these fees into your pricing strategy so that you're still making a profit.

To set the price for your digital product on Etsy, simply enter the price in the *Price* section of the listing form. Be sure to choose a price that accurately reflects the value of your product and takes into account the factors listed above.

To be honest, at the end of the day, the price you can charge for your products is dependent on what the competition is charging. Digital products are a highly competitive category on Etsy. So while you may feel that your products are worth a lot of money, if other sellers are charging $.99 for their coloring book pages, you will likely have to match their price.

Selling digital products is all about volume. Unlike selling a unique handmade necklace or a one-of-a-kind vintage vase, digital downloads are products that can be replicated thousands of times. You can charge more for unique art downloads or customized products. But if you are selling products such as coloring pages that are the same for every customer, you aren't going to be able to charge a lot of money. However, as you start getting orders, your listing will start to gain traction on Etsy, and you will earn more money based on the volume of orders.

A 99-cent digital download will net you a profit of 46 cents. However, if you sell 1000 files, you will earn $460. 10,000 files would earn you $4,600. Since you only create the file once and can list it to automatically renew every four months, you will earn passive income on that one listing for as long as it is on Etsy. The more products you have listed, the more likely you are to have sales. More listings equal more sales, which eventually leads to a steady stream of passive income!

Quantity: Unlike a physical product where you have a set quantity of an item, digital products can be downloaded an infinite number of times. The maximum quantity you can list an item on Etsy is 999. I recommend listing 999 as your quantity for every digital download you offer. If you have automatic renewal on, it will never go out of stock unless you sell more than 999 in four months.

Allow restock requests: *Allow Restock Requests* is an option available to sellers on Etsy that allows buyers to request notification when an item that is currently out of stock becomes available again. When this option is enabled, buyers can choose to receive an email notification when the seller updates the listing to indicate that the item is back in stock. If a buyer requests a restock notification for an out-of-stock item, the seller will receive a message notifying them of the request. The seller can then update the listing and Etsy will notify the buyer that it is back in stock.

Variations: The *Variations* section in an Etsy listing allows sellers to offer multiple versions or options of a product within a single listing. For example, some sellers may have several different color schemes for the same digital download. Rather than creating a separate listing for each color, they can create variations for the different colors.

Another use for this section is to offer variations of the number of files someone can buy. Using our coloring book example, you could create individual variations for each page and then a variation to buy all 10. By listing the pages at a low price and then offering the set for a discount over purchasing the pages separately, it can encourage customers to pay more for the bundle.

Personalization: If you plan to offer customization of your digital downloads, you will first need to make sure you've selected *Made To Order* in the *About This Listing* section of the listing form. Etsy will then walk you through the steps needed to provide custom files to your customers.

When you enable *Personalization* in your listings, Etsy will prompt you to provide **Instructions for buyers**. Remember that when you offer personalization, you'll need to provide an updated file to your customer. When a buyer purchases an as-is product, such as coloring book pages, they'll receive the digital file immediately. If the personalization option is enabled, you'll receive specific instructions from the customer regarding how they want to personalize the product. You'll then need to create a customized file for the customer and upload it to Etsy. Once you upload the completed file, Etsy will automatically transfer it to the buyer. Only then will you receive payment.

It's important to note that the process of providing personalized files can take longer than delivering non-personalized files, so it's a good idea to manage your customers' expectations regarding the turnaround time. In listings for personalized products, be sure to extend the handling time to accommodate the time you will need to customize orders. If you know it will only take you two days to complete a custom order, make your handling time four days. That way you are covered in case of an emergency. And if you deliver the file faster, the customer will be happy.

Shipping: When you select *Digital* rather than *Physical* under *Type*, Etsy will automatically remove the physical shipping options from your listing. Not having to worry about shipping is the best part of selling digital products!

Digital Files: This is the section where you upload your PDF or other files. You can add up to six files within one listing. Remember that if you offer personalization, you would have needed to select *Made To Order* under the *About This Listing* section at the start of the listing. Etsy will walk you through the steps needed to upload and complete the order.

Remember that as this is a beginners' guide, we've focused mainly on products that you will deliver as a PDF file. If you have the option to offer your products in other formats, go ahead and add additional options. For example, you can download Canva files as PDF but also JPG and PNG. There are no additional fees to upload other file options, so if you have them available, go ahead and do so.

Returns and exchanges: According to Etsy, "Digital items aren't eligible for returns or exchanges on Etsy because of the nature of these items." This is another great benefit of selling digital downloads! However, Etsy does note that if there is a problem with the product in that it doesn't match the listing photo or description a customer can file a complaint to get a refund.

Publish: And that's it! Your first listing is done! You can click on *Preview* to see how it will look to shoppers, or you can go ahead and click *Publish* to make it live on Etsy's website. You can edit your listing at any time once it is live. And if you panic and decide you don't want it listed, you can easily end it. However, once you hit *Publish*, you will be charged the $.40 listing fee. If you end the listing early, you will not get a partial refund of the listing fee.

Creating Your Second Listing: Once your first listing is done, you can get started creating your second listing! My tip is to go to your *Seller Dashboard* and click on *Listings*. However, rather than click on *+ Add* a listing, go to your first listing, and click on the little screw icon. A drop-down menu will appear. Select *Copy*, and Etsy will create a copy of that listing that you can then edit.

This *Copy* option is also known as the *Sell Similar* technique in which you simply make a copy of an existing listing and edit the details. This saves you a lot of time versus creating every single listing from scratch. And if you stick to doing similar listings in batches, it will go even faster. Using our coloring book example, if you are listing other coloring books, list them one after the other using the *Copy* feature so that you will have minimal fields to edit.

The Hard Truth: When selling digital products, it's common to have about 20% of your listings generate the majority of your sales, with the remaining 80% either selling very little or not at all. While this may seem disheartening, the advantage of selling digital products is that it costs very little to create and list the items, so you won't be losing much money if some products don't sell. As your business grows, you will be able to identify which products sell well and can focus on creating more products similar to those. You will also learn which products to avoid, saving you time and effort.

Etsy SEO: We've touched on Etsy SEO several times throughout this chapter, but I want to take some more time here to cover it fully because it is so important to building a successful business.

Etsy SEO refers to *Search Engine Optimization,* which is the process of optimizing your Etsy shop and product listings to improve their visibility in Etsy search results. When someone searches for a product on Etsy, the platform's search algorithm analyzes the product titles, descriptions, tags, and shop sections to determine the most relevant results to show to the searcher. The more you overlap your best keywords, the more you are telling Etsy that they should be focused on those keywords. Optimizing these areas in your listings with relevant keywords and phrases can help them appear higher in search results and reach more potential customers.

To optimize your Etsy SEO, be sure to conduct keyword research to identify the words and phrases that your target customers are likely to use when searching for products like yours. As I've mentioned, I use both eRank.com and EtsyCheck.com to research the best keywords for my listings. I use these keywords in my listing titles, descriptions, tags, and shop sections.

In addition to using the most relevant keywords throughout my listings, I also ensure that my listings are filled out and that I am using high-quality photos. Additionally, you may want to consider optimizing other elements of your shop, such as your shop name and *About* section, which can also help improve your visibility in search results.

Overall, Etsy SEO is all about understanding your target customers and using relevant keywords and high-quality content to help your products stand out in search results and attract more buyers to your shop. While it sounds complex, the fact is that it is more tedious than difficult. And while you may be tempted to skip focusing on SEO altogether to save time, the fact is that Etsy's algorithm relies heavily on SEO, more so than any other website. So if you want to build a successful Etsy shop, you have to focus on SEO. The good news is that the more you work on SEO, the more natural the process will become for you. You may even find that you stop relying on keyword research as you instinctively know what terms to use to maximize your sales.

CHAPTER SIX: MANAGING YOUR ETSY SHOP

Managing your Etsy shop is a crucial part of running a successful online business. While selling digital products is one of the most passive business models there is, you still need to attend to your shop regularly if you want to grow and make more money. Whether it's listing new products, editing existing ones, updating the look of your storefront, or answering customer questions, there are plenty of things to keep you busy as a shop owner.

Running an Etsy digital shop isn't just about making sales; it's about ensuring that your customers have a positive experience from start to finish. When you manage your Etsy shop effectively, you can build a loyal customer base and stand out from the competition with a strong record of sales and positive reviews.

Here are some tips for managing your Etsy shop:

Shop Policies: One of the most important aspects of managing your Etsy shop is setting up clear shop policies. Your shop policies should be easy to understand and communicate what customers can expect when they purchase from you. For a digital download business, the most important shop policies include:

Delivery and processing times: Your shop policies should include information on how quickly customers can expect to receive their digital products after purchase. For non-personalized products, your customers will receive their files from Etsy immediately after their payment clears. If you are offering personalization, you will need time to customize orders. Therefore, you will need to provide a clear processing time to create the product and deliver it to the customer.

Refunds and exchanges: As we've already discussed, Etsy does not allow refunds or exchanges on digital products unless there is a problem with the item. However, if you are offering personalization, you will want to set a time for buyers to cancel an order. Once you start making a custom order, it will be too late for a buyer to cancel. Since most cancellations come within an hour of an order being placed, you should wait at least an hour before you start working on an order. By clearly stating your timeframe in your listing, you will be able to protect yourself from cancellations that come in after you've already finished a custom order.

Technical support: Not everyone is familiar with digital downloads and the nature of printable products, so you will need to be prepared to have to explain to customers exactly how they will receive their order and then print it out on their end. Putting this information in your item descriptions will go a long way toward educating customers about how to open and print out the files you are selling. Etsy will also provide your customers with information when they receive their files.

However, no matter how many times you put instructions in your listings and messages, you will still get messages from some customers who need more direction (or who just didn't read your listing). Having a set of directions saved in a Word document that you can copy and paste in response to any questions makes it easy to answer messages about how to download files. Etsy is very strict about answering messages, so responding to inquiries quickly is very important. I keep my instructions both on my computer and on my smartphone so I can send them to customers no matter where I am.

Copyright and licensing: Your shop policies should outline the copyright and licensing terms for your digital products. This may include information on whether customers can use the products for personal or commercial purposes, as well as any restrictions or limitations on use. Adding a copyright message in small print at the bottom of your products is also advisable unless you are creating a personalized product.

Listing management: Unless you are selling personalized products, your digital product sales will usually occur seamlessly. The customer will place their order and Etsy will deliver the file to them once their payment clears. To avoid issues with customers, you want to manage your listings effectively, including:

- **Accurate listings:** Your digital product listings should be clear, concise, and accurate. Customers should be able to understand what they are buying, what they can expect to receive, and how to use the product. Use descriptive language, high-quality images, and clearly state any limitations or restrictions on the product's use to avoid issues after the sale.

- **Proper categorization:** Make sure that you choose the appropriate categories and subcategories for your digital product listings. Remember that you can choose one main category as well as additional subcategories. Let Etsy show you the available options based on a search of what your product is. A tip is to vary your categories for the same product types to get them into multiple categories, which will help bring in more customers.

- **Consistent branding:** Use consistent branding across your listings, including in the look of your photos, titles, and descriptions. When you look at your Etsy storefront, you want all of your listings to have a cohesive look. And you want to extend your brand's look to your social media pages, too, by using the same profile picture and banners across all platforms.

- **Regular updating:** Regularly update your Etsy product listings to ensure that they remain relevant and accurate. Update the product descriptions, images, and titles as necessary to reflect any changes or updates to the product. If you haven't had any sales for months, re-evaluate the listing to see if there is anything you can make better, such as new photos or a better title. And be sure to delete listings that haven't sold in over a year. You don't want unsold items clogging up your shop when you can list new products that might sell better.

- **Pricing Strategy:** Set a pricing strategy that is competitive and reflects the value of your products. Remember that the digital product market on Etsy is very competitive, and the amount you can charge for your products is going to depend on what other sellers are pricing their items at. Once an item becomes a best-seller, you can bump up the price a bit. But when you are starting, it's more important to get those first sales than it is to make a big profit. And if that means you have to sell downloads for $.99 just to get your foot in the door, then so be it. You can always raise prices later.

Order management: Order management refers to the process of managing orders from the time they are received until they are fulfilled and delivered to the customer. As we've established, unless you are selling personalized products, most digital downloads will go directly to your customer immediately after they order, meaning you won't have contact with the buyer. There is nothing for you to package and ship, which is one of the best parts of this business model.

However, if you are selling personalized digital files, you will need to keep on top of orders and do the following:

- **Order fulfillment:** When you receive an order for a personalized digital product, make sure that you fulfill it promptly according to the processing time you set in your listing. I always believe in exceeding expectations by under-promising and over-delivering. If your listing states you will fulfill orders in five days, aim for three.

- **Customization options:** Make sure that you spell out in the listing itself about what customization options are included. Also, provide clear instructions on how customers can provide their personalization details for you. Etsy will provide a section for you to fill out when you list custom products, but make sure instructions are in your listing's description, too.

- **Communication:** Communication is key when managing orders in your Etsy shop. Respond promptly to customer inquiries and keep buyers informed about the status of their orders. Etsy has strict guidelines for answering messages, so be sure to check for incoming messages at least twice a day. Failure to reply promptly can affect your seller ranking.

- **Quality Control:** Before delivering custom digital products to customers, double-check to make sure there are no errors. If a customer replies that you have, in fact, made a mistake, apologize and work to fix it quickly.

Stats: In your *Shop Manager* you will find a tab for *Stats*. Here you will find data that includes the following:

- **Visits:** How many people visited your shop
- **Orders:** How many orders your shop had
- **Conversion Rate:** How many shop visitors made a purchase. The average is between 2% to 3%, so anything above that means you are doing better than most!
- **Revenue:** Your gross sales before Etsy takes out fees

You can sort the above data by various date ranges, including:

- **Today**
- **Yesterday**
- **Last 7 Days**
- **Last 30 Days**
- **This Month**
- **This Year**
- **Last Year**
- **All Time**

- **Custom**

You can also compare the data to the previous period. By analyzing these numbers, you can see if your shop is growing or if you are stagnant. You can also compare seasonal sales of items to know if you should create more of a certain product for upcoming holidays or cut back on your offerings. I find comparing my current year-to-date over last year's numbers is a good way to see if I am growing, am stagnant, or worse, am seeing a decline in sales.

How shoppers found you: In addition to the information mentioned earlier, the *Stats* section also provides detailed insights into the sources of your shop's traffic. The columns in this section provide a breakdown of where your customers found your listings.

Etsy provides two main categories for traffic sources: Etsy and non-Etsy. Etsy refers to the percentage of visits that your shop received from within Etsy, such as through Etsy search or Etsy marketing programs. Non-Etsy traffic, on the other hand, includes visits from external sources such as social media, search engines, and other websites.

By reviewing these traffic source statistics, you can gain valuable insights into the effectiveness of your marketing efforts. For example, if a majority of your traffic is coming from within Etsy, it indicates that your product listings are optimized for Etsy search and/or that your Etsy ads are effective, both of which are great.

However, it also means that you have an opportunity to bring in even more customers by working harder on bringing in your own traffic from social media.

Alternatively, if most of your traffic is coming from you driving your traffic to your shop via social media, it might indicate that you need to work on your Etsy SEO and/or run Etsy ads to gain more customers who are already shopping on the site. Etsy will show you how your numbers compare to the same period last year, which helps you further narrow down where your marketing efforts may be falling short.

See traffic and sales driven by Offsite Ads: Another helpful section under *Stats* is where Etsy breaks down your offsite ads, which are ads placed on Google, Instagram, Facebook, Pinterest, and Bing. Remember that if you sell less than $10,000 in a year that offsite ads are optional. For sellers who make over $10,000 a year, enrollment is mandatory. However, you only pay for offsite ads when they lead to a sale.

The fee you pay for each sale through an offsite ad is high at 15%, but I believe that any sale is a good sale as it increases the rank of your listing. Etsy will show you how many times shoppers clicked on an offsite ad and how many orders were placed. They will also show you which items sold, how much you earned, and how much you paid in fees.

Shopper Views of Listings: Also under *Stats*, Etsy will show you how many people viewed each of your listings along with other actions shoppers took. They will break this data down into:

- **Views:** How many people looked at each of your listings
- **Favorites:** How many people favored each of your listings
- **Orders:** How many of each listing, if any, were ordered
- **Revenue:** How much money, if any, you earned from each listing

This is a helpful section as you can see exactly how many views each listing is getting. If you see that listings aren't getting any views, you should take some time to edit those listings to improve their photos, titles, descriptions, and tags, and maybe even change your pricing.

Organization: Organization is essential for running any business, including a successful Etsy digital shop. While digital products don't create the type of clutter other businesses deal with (there is little to no paper, there are no packing materials, and all of your storage is on your computer), they do require a lot of computer files, including product files, photos, graphics, and more.

Starting with a system of organizing your digital files will save you time and frustration as your shop grows. You might create a folder for each product line or a folder for each type of file. If you sell coloring pages, for example, you might create folders for each niche you sell. Within each niche, you would then store graphics related to those products.

When I started my shop, I had one single file folder on my computer where I stored all files in. It quickly became overrun with hundreds of images and templates, leaving me overwhelmed. I had to painstakingly go through every single file and move it to a new dedicated folder. It took me hours to reorganize everything. Don't make the same mistake I did: start with a folder system right away!

Time Management: Time management is crucial for any business, and while selling digital products can eventually turn into a form of semi-passive income, there is a lot of work to get an Etsy shop up and running. From creating new products and listing them to answering customer questions and working on marketing, there is always something to do.

Here are some tips for maintaining a healthy work-life balance:

1. **Set a schedule:** It can be tempting to work on your Etsy shop at all hours of the day, but it's important to set a schedule and stick to it. This will help you avoid burnout and ensure that you have time for the personal aspects of your life. While Etsy shoppers are online 24/7, that doesn't mean that you need to be stuck at your computer around the clock. I break up my workday so that I'm in my office off and on

throughout the day. I tend to work an hour in the morning, an hour in the afternoon, and then an hour in the evening.

2. **Prioritize tasks:** Make a list of tasks you need to accomplish each day or week and prioritize them based on urgency and importance. This will help you stay focused and ensure that you're making progress on the most critical tasks. Remember that creating new products and listings is the most important thing you need to do to grow your business. If you can, aim to list at least one new product every day.

3. **Automate where possible:** Look for ways to automate certain tasks, such as social media posts or email responses. This can save you time and allow you to focus on other areas of your business. Almost all social media platforms allow you to schedule posts. And Etsy offers automated response messaging that you can set up to answer commonly asked questions before you can get back to a customer personally.

4. **Outsource when needed:** If you find yourself overwhelmed or struggling to keep up with certain tasks, consider outsourcing them to a freelancer or virtual assistant. Figure out what part of your business you excel at and enjoy and try to figure out a way to deal with the tasks you don't. If you have a teenager in your life, consider hiring them to handle some of your social media tasks. If you find that

creating custom products is too taxing for you, switch to offering products that don't require personalization.

5. **Take breaks:** It can be easy to get caught up in your work and forget to take breaks, but it's important to step away from your computer and take time for yourself. This will help you avoid burnout and stay motivated in the long run, especially if you are having a sales slump or dealing with a string of difficult customers. If you are feeling overwhelmed or burned out, put your Etsy shop on vacation for a couple of days.

CHAPTER SEVEN: HANDLING CUSTOMER SERVICE ISSUES

While running an Etsy digital product shop can be profitable and fun, operating any business is not all sunshine and rainbows. As much as you may love creating and selling your digital products to customers all over the world and building a semi-passive stream of income, we all know that sometimes things can go wrong. Maybe a customer is having trouble downloading their purchase, or maybe they're unhappy with the product they received. Whatever the issue may be, it's important to handle it to ensure that your customers are satisfied and that your shop's reputation remains intact.

In this chapter, we'll explore the ins and outs of handling customer service issues in an Etsy digital product shop. We'll cover everything from how to communicate effectively with customers to how to resolve disputes and prevent negative feedback.

Common types of customer service issues on Etsy: When it comes to running an Etsy digital product shop, customer service issues can come in all shapes and sizes. From technical difficulties with downloading products to misunderstandings about what's included in the purchase, dealing with these issues can be frustrating, especially if you know you are in the right. However, it's important to remain calm and handle all issues professionally.

Here are some of the most common types of customer service issues that you may encounter in your digital product shop:

Technical issues: Customers may have trouble downloading their files or printing out their products. This may be caused by technical glitches or compatibility issues with the customer's device or software. Make sure that you provide clear and concise instructions for customers on the technical requirements of your files in your listings. Also highlight terms such as "PDF," "digital files," and "printables." You can even include, "This is a digital file that you will have to download to your computer and print yourself."

Offer a step-by-step checklist of how to download and print the files that you include in the listing and an automatic message to all buyers. But whatever you do, make sure you keep all messaging between you and your buyers through Etsy's messaging system. If a buyer asks you to email them a file, do not do it. Instead, report the issue to Etsy directly to have them intervene. All file transfers need to go through Etsy's system. Sending files outside of Etsy cancels out your seller protections.

Product dissatisfaction: Despite your best efforts, some customers may be dissatisfied with their digital products. This can be due to a variety of reasons, such as a mismatch between the product description and what they received or unexpected limitations on the product's use.

Perhaps you sold one coloring page but the customer thought there were buying a set. Or maybe you sold a planner sheet in a certain shade of blue but your customer's printer doesn't match what they see on the screen. As I've already noted, shoppers are notorious for not reading listing descriptions. But as long as you have accurately represented your product in your photos, titles, and descriptions, Etsy will back you up.

Here are some best practices for addressing product satisfaction issues:

1. **Listen to the customer:** When a customer expresses dissatisfaction with a product, you want to listen to their concerns and try to understand their perspective. Ask questions to clarify the issue and show that you're committed to trying to resolve things. I typically say something like, "I'm so sorry to hear there is an issue with your order. What can I do to make things right?"

2. **Offer solutions:** Based on the customer's concerns, offer solutions that can help address the issue. Remember that sales of digital files on Etsy are final, but if you genuinely made a mistake, issue the customer a refund. If the error was on the buyer, politely show them that the product

listing indeed matches the product sold. If they continue to press for a refund, ask the customer to reach out to Etsy so that Etsy can step in and resolve the issue without you continue engaging with the customer.

3. **Apologize and take responsibility:** Everyone makes mistakes, and if you accidentally misrepresented a product, it's important to apologize and take responsibility for the situation by supplying a corrected file or issuing the buyer a full refund.

4. **Revise product descriptions:** If customers are consistently experiencing product dissatisfaction due to a mismatch between the product description and what they received, revise your product descriptions to be more accurate and detailed. By providing as much detail as possible, you will protect yourself from future issues as Etsy will back you up in cases where customers simply didn't read the listing.

Payment and refund Issues: Payment processing and refund requests can be another source of customer service issues. For example, a customer may have been overcharged or mistakenly charged multiple times for the same purchase. Because Etsy handles all payment processing, including refunds, you need to direct buyers to contact Etsy to resolve any issues. There is nothing you as an Etsy seller can do regarding payment processing.

Communication: Lack of communication and responsiveness can be a source of customer service issues. Customers may feel frustrated if they don't receive prompt responses to their inquiries or if they feel that their concerns are not being taken seriously. Common issues include delayed or unresponsive communication from the seller, vague or unhelpful responses to customer inquiries, poor communication about delivery times, or just plain rudeness.

To address communication and responsiveness issues, aim for the following:

1. **Respond promptly:** When a customer reaches out to you with a question or concern, make sure to respond as quickly as possible. You can access Etsy messages on your computer or smartphone. The faster you respond, the more reassurance the customer will feel that their concerns are being taken seriously.

2. **Use professional language:** When communicating with customers, make sure to use clear and professional language that's easy to understand. Avoid using jargon or technical terms that may be confusing to the customer. Don't match a customer's negativity. Don't use profanity or show frustration. Respond the way you hope a seller would respond to you if you reached out with an issue.

3. **Provide accurate information:** When providing information to customers, make sure that it's accurate and up to date.

This can help prevent confusion or misunderstandings down the line. Again, make sure instructions regarding the system requirements and download instructions are spelled out in your listings and in responses to questions.

Setting up shop policies: One of the most important aspects of running an Etsy digital product shop is setting up shop policies to manage expectations for customers and establish guidelines for resolving disputes. Your shop policies should be clear, concise, and easy to understand. They should address common issues that customers may encounter, such as download and technical issues, product satisfaction, and communication and responsiveness.

Here are some key elements to consider when setting up shop policies:

1. **Technical Issues:** Clearly state how you will handle download and technical issues, including the steps customers should take to resolve the issue and the timeline for resolution. Offer specific steps for customers to download, edit, and print the downloads they purchase from you. Keeping these steps written out in a Word document that you can copy and paste into your listings and in messages is a quick and easy way to resolve these issues.

2. **Product satisfaction:** As we've noted, Etsy doesn't allow you to create a refund or exchange policy in listings for digital

products, but if the product itself is flawed or you are late in the delivery of a custom product, you will need to make it right with the customer. In my policies, I state that all sales are final unless an item is not as described.

3. **Delivery:** If you offer customized digital products, clearly state how long it will take you to create and deliver files. As I've mentioned before, under promise and overdeliver. If your policy state that you will deliver customized products within five days, make sure to deliver the files in under three days. This will result in happy customers who will leave you positive reviews and hopefully come back to buy from you again.

Creating a FAQ page: An FAQ (Frequently Asked Questions) section is an easy way to address common questions and concerns that your customers may have about your digital products and shop policies. By providing clear and concise answers to frequently asked questions, you can save time and reduce the number of messages you receive from customers.

You can include an FAQ section in your shop announcement by adding a heading and a list of questions and answers. This will be visible on your shop homepage. You can also add frequently asked questions to the description of each product you sell. This way, customers will have access to information that is specific to each product.

Here are some tips for creating effective FAQs for your Etsy digital product shop:

1. **Identify common questions:** Review the most common questions and concerns that customers have about your digital products and shop policies. These may include questions about product features, the differences between the files you offer, how to edit the files, and how to print out the files.

2. **Keep it simple:** When creating your FAQ section, make sure that the language is simple and easy to understand. Avoid using technical terms or jargon that may be confusing to your customers. State the file types you offer, how customers can easily download them, if customers can edit the files, and how they can print them.

3. **Provide detailed answers:** For each question, provide a detailed and comprehensive answer that addresses all aspects of the question. Not all customers understand how easy it is to open, download, and print files. While it may see easy to you, explain it thoroughly to customers. This can help prevent follow-up questions and reduce customer frustration.

4. **Keep it up to date:** Review your FAQ section regularly to ensure that the information is accurate and up to date. If you make changes to your shop policies or products, make

sure to update your FAQ section accordingly. For example, maybe you started your business not offering customization options but as your business grew, you began offering to personalize files, meaning you need to provide a whole new set of FAQs that reflect your new product offerings.

Answering messages: Etsy's policy for responding to customer messages is to do so promptly within 24 hours. According to Etsy's seller guidelines, "sellers are expected to respond to messages from customers promptly to ensure a positive experience and to maintain good customer service." While Etsy's policy is to answer messages within 24 hours, it's best to reply as soon as you can, ideally within a few hours.

Stay professional: No matter how hard you work to give your customers a top-notch experience with both your products and service, you can't please everyone all of the time. Eventually, someone will contact you upset about an order. While it's hard to remain calm when someone lashes out at you, you want to stay calm and professional. The following tips may help:

1. **Stay calm and be polite:** It's important to remain calm and polite when responding to customers, even ones who may be rude or aggressive. Avoid getting defensive or argumentative, as this can make the situation worse. Instead, take a deep breath and respond calmly and

professionally. Often customers enter into conversations with sellers expecting a fight. By showing sympathy for their situation, even if they are in the wrong, you can usually calm them down.

2. **Acknowledge their concerns:** Even if the customer is being rude, try to focus on the underlying issue that they are upset about. Acknowledge their concerns and let them know that you understand their frustration. Most issues are a result of customers not reading the listing description of the item they bought. By gently directing them to the description and reminding them that Etsy's policy is that all digital sales are final, you can hopefully diffuse the situation.

3. **Offer a solution:** If possible, offer a solution to the customer's problem. Etsy does not allow refunds or exchanges on digital products, so if a customer simply has buyer's remorse, you should stick to your policies. If they made a genuine mistake, rather than issuing them a refund (because once they've downloaded the file, they can't return it), you could offer them a coupon code to save money on their next order from you.

4. **Set boundaries:** If the customer continues to be rude or becomes threatening, it's important to set boundaries to protect yourself and your shop. Let them know that while you understand their frustration, it is against Etsy's policies

for buyers to use abusive language. If a buyer continues to attack you through messages, stop communicating with them and escalate the issue to Etsy's customer support team.

5. **Only communicate through Etsy:** Do not communicate with customers outside of Etsy. Your conversations through Etsy's messaging system are saved and can be seen by Etsy's support team if you need to report a threatening customer. Do not reply to customers who email you directly as doing so will cancel out your seller protections.

Automatic Message Response: Utilizing Etsy's automatic response feature is a great way to keep on top of messages if you are away from your office for four hours or more. An automatic response counts as a response, giving you time to get back to your computer to answer questions directly while still meeting Etsy's timeframe.

Your automatic response should be clear, concise, and professional. Let customers know you are temporarily away from your desk but will answer them shortly. The easiest way to answer most questions is to include your shop FAQ in your automatic responses. This will hopefully answer most questions or at least keep customers happy until you can reply directly.

To set up automatic replies:

1. Log in to your Etsy account and go to your **Seller Dashboard**.

2. Click on **Messages** in the left-hand menu.

3. Click on **Auto Reply** in the top-right corner of the screen.

4. Under the Auto-reply section, select either *Temporary Auto-Reply* or *Weekly Auto-Reply*.

5. *Temporary Auto-Reply* allows you to set up replies if you plan to be away for 1 hour, 4 hours, 12 hours, 1 day, 2 days, 3 days, 4 days, or 5 days.

6. *Weekly Auto-Reply* allows you to set your business hours so customers will know when you are in the office. For example, you can set your hours as Monday through Friday from 8 am to 5 pm.

7. Follow the prompts to set up your automatic reply message and schedule.

8. **Save your settings**. Once you've set up your automatic replies, they will be sent to customers who message you during the designated time frame.

Understanding Etsy's policies and procedures: Etsy has specific policies and guidelines in place for digital downloads that can be helpful when dealing with customer service issues. Here are some of Etsy's policies related to digital downloads:

1. **Instant downloads:** Etsy requires that all digital products listed for sale in the marketplace be available as instant

downloads unless the seller specifies that they offer personalization. This means that customers should be able to download their purchased digital products immediately after their payment clears. Unless you are selling custom products, you have to upload the digital download when you create the listing, making it ready for customers to download immediately upon purchase.

2. **File types and formats:** Etsy allows a variety of file types and formats for digital products, but sellers are responsible for ensuring that their products are compatible with the platforms and software specified in their product descriptions. Most sellers offer PDF files for their printable products. Graphics, however, are usually JPG or PNG files. You want to offer the most commonly used files that the vast majority of computer users will be able to download, open, and print.

3. **File delivery:** If you are selling custom downloads, you must deliver the files to your customer within the stated timeframe. Failure to do so can result in Etsy canceling the sale and automatically issuing the customer a refund. Give yourself plenty of time to fulfill orders, doing your best to fulfill them earlier than stated. As I've already mentioned, I use the "under promise and over delivery" approach, stating

I will deliver products within a longer timeframe than I end up using.

4. **Refunds and exchanges:** Etsy only allows for refunds and exchanges for digital products under certain circumstances. For example, if the product is defective, not as described, or doesn't work as intended. Otherwise, all digital sales are final. Being able to tell customers that this is Etsy's policy, not yours, helps protect you from customers who demand refunds. After all, once a customer downloads a file, they can't return it to you. Refunding their money would still mean they keep the file.

CHAPTER EIGHT: ADVERTISING & MARKETING YOUR PRODUCTS

As we've discussed several times throughout this book, when you begin the process of starting an Etsy shop, one of the first things you will hear is the term **SEO, or Search Engine Optimization.** Remember that SEO refers to the practice of optimizing your online content so that it is more visible and easily discoverable by search engines like Google. In other words, repeating relevant keywords in your titles, descriptions, tags, and shop sections tells Etsy that they need to focus on those keywords when putting your items into their search algorithm.

When done effectively, SEO can help your products to rank higher in search results and increase the chances of them being seen by potential customers. And effective use of Etsy can eliminate the need to run expensive Etsy Ads. Once I mastered Etsy SEO, I stopped using Etsy Ads, which are the ads you pay for whenever someone clicks on them. I do opt into Etsy Off-Site Ads as I only pay for those ads when a click leads to a sale.

It can't be said enough that SEO is the number one tool you must utilize to bring customers to your Etsy shop. Remember that SEO boils down to the use of keywords, both in your shop and in your listings. Researching the best keywords for your products and using those keywords in your titles, descriptions, tags, shop sections, and even in areas where you can customize your shop's announcements and information will tell Etsy that they need to be pushing your products to customers searching those keywords.

Is it annoying that you can't just write a good title and be done with the listing? Yes. It is tempting to just focus on a keyword-loaded title and call it a day the same way Amazon, eBay, and Poshmark sellers do with their listings? Yes. But unfortunately, this isn't the reality of selling on Etsy. Repeating the most important keywords that pertain to your listings is the best thing you can do to bring shoppers to your listings and turn those shoppers into paying customers.

But while SEO is a huge part of customers finding your products when they are searching Etsy or Google, there are other things you can do to bring traffic to your Etsy shop. And fortunately, most of these things are not only relatively easy but also free. That's because these tactics mostly involve utilizing social media platforms to grow your business.

When e-commerce was still in its initial stages, there were very few shopping websites and customers were limited in where they could buy things online. When I began selling online, the only online retailers were eBay and Amazon. For years, I sold on both sites successfully. Because customers only had eBay and Amazon to shop on, I didn't have to compete for shoppers. The customers who were shopping online came to me because they didn't have anywhere else to go. I didn't even have to have the best pictures, titles, or descriptions because there was very little competition.

However, the e-commerce landscape has changed significantly since I began selling online in 2005. There are now thousands of online shopping websites available. Every single brand and retail store has its e-commerce website, and numerous "reselling" platforms have emerged, including Etsy, Poshmark, Mercari, Facebook Marketplace, TikTok Shops, and WhatNot. This increase in competition means that simply listing products for sale is no longer enough to make sales.

Etsy is an especially competitive marketplace. It is no longer just for crafters and vintage sellers. Sticker shops, print-on-demand drop shipping, and now digital downloads are all a huge part of Etsy's offerings. That means that you as a seller are not only competing against other digital product shops but all of the other shops on Etsy. For instance, if you sell digital planners, you will be competing with other digital planner shops and with shops that sell planner products that they print and ship to their customers.

Because so many people are now selling on Etsy, it is important to think of your Etsy shop as a brand. The category and niches you focus on, the digital products you create for your shop, and the aesthetic of your items should all have a cohesive look and theme that contributes to your brand identity. If your shop offers digital wedding invitations, you'll be using white, silver, and gold colors for not only your products but also the overall look of your shop. If you are selling children's activity book downloads, you will likely use bright primary colors.

Once you have mastered Etsy SEO and have done all you can to bring in shoppers who are already on Etsy, you can turn your attention to bringing in customers from other websites. And the first place you will want to start is on Facebook.

Facebook: If you want to grow a successful Etsy shop of any kind, creating a Facebook page is essential. With nearly 3 billion registered users, there's no better place to find new customers than on Facebook. Fortunately, Facebook is not only free but easy to use. And while other social media platforms such as TikTok are gaining traction, Facebook is still the number one social media site for businesses.

To utilize Facebook to bring customers to your Etsy shop, you will need to create a **Facebook Business Page**, which is different from a personal account. With a personal Facebook account, friends and family send you "friend requests." You can make your account completely private, and you don't have to edit yourself as your posts will only be seen by those who you approve as "friends."

However, a *Facebook Business Page* is different than a personal account as rather than people "friending" you, they will instead need to "like" your page to "follow" you. You need this distinction to separate your personal life from your business, not only to build your brand but to protect your privacy. While you may enjoy discussing politics and religion on your personal Facebook page, you want to refrain from these sometimes-controversial topics when it comes to your business.

You can use a *Facebook Business Page* to promote your products, share updates about your business, and interact with your customers. It is easy to link to your Etsy shop on your Facebook page so that users can easily access your listings. By building a following on Facebook and actively engaging with your audience, you can drive traffic to your Etsy shop and increase sales.

To create a *Facebook Business Page,* follow these simple steps:

1. Go to facebook.com/about/pages
2. Log in to your personal Facebook account
3. Follow the prompts to create a new business page

The first decision you will need to make is to name your page. I currently have several Facebook pages, including one for my Etsy

Shop. My Facebook page name is Jean Lee Publishing, which matches my Etsy Shop name.

As you create additional social media accounts related to your Etsy business, it's important to make sure that they all have the same name to establish a cohesive online presence. You will want all your social media account names to match or closely match your Etsy shop name.

For example, I sell journals, planners, notebooks, and adult coloring books on Amazon through their self-publishing platform, Amazon KDP. My pen name for those products is Jean Lee Publishing. I decided to name my Etsy shop the same so that I could create different products under one pen name, which has enabled me to have a dedicated website where customers can choose to visit my Etsy shop or Amazon storefront.

The biggest benefit of having this one brand name is that it allows me to have one social media handle for both platforms. Since all of my products fall under the "stationery" category, it made sense for me to focus on combing all of my items together under one name. By directing customers to www.JeanLeePublishing.com, they can see all of the stationery products I sell and click through to the ones they are most interested in.

After you have created a Facebook business account, Facebook will prompt you to personalize your page by:

1. **Adding a profile picture:** This is the main image that will appear next to your page name and posts. I advise that you use the same profile picture for your Facebook page that you use for your Etsy shop. Most Etsy sellers choose their shop's logo as their profile picture.

2. **Adding a banner:** This is the large image that appears at the top of your Facebook page. You can use a custom banner that you have designed or made on a site like Fiverr.com, or you can create your graphics using tools like Canva or WordSwag. Just as you want your profile picture to be the same across your Etsy shop and all social media accounts, it's also a good idea to make your Facebook banner match or closely match the one in your Etsy shop.

3. **Customizing your page's tabs:** Facebook allows you to add various tabs to your page, such as an events calendar or a shop tab. You can customize these tabs to suit your business and make it easier for users to find the information they are looking for.

It's important to complete the **About** section on your Facebook business page to provide visitors with more information about your Etsy shop. Here you can include more details about your products, target audience, and even why you started your business in the first place. However, be mindful not to post personal information on your business page.

For example, while you may want to include your phone number on your personal page so that friends and family can contact you, you won't want to include it on your business page unless you have a brick-and-mortar location that you want customers to visit or call. For an Etsy digital download shop, your entire business is online through Etsy. Therefore, there is no need for anyone to call you. The only place you want customers to visit or message you through is your Etsy shop.

Page Category: Several categories may be relevant for an Etsy digital shop on Facebook, and Facebook allows you to select three for your business page. I recommend the following:

1. **Product/Service**
2. **Shopping & Retail**
3. **Arts & Crafts**

While *Product/Service* is the most important category you want to choose, you also want to choose two additional categories so that your Facebook page is visible to as many people as possible. The goal is to get Facebook users to "like" your page. And when they "like" your page, Facebook will then show their friends and family your page. This method of gaining followers through "likes" is how you build your Facebook following, which will then translate into bringing more people to your Etsy shop. Note that you can also change categories at any time if necessary.

Once you've chosen your page's categories, you will want to personalize your Facebook business page by editing the URL to reflect the name of your page. Remember that you want to name your page the same as your Etsy shop or close to it. This will make it easier for users to find and follow your page, as well as establish a cohesive online presence.

To **change the username** of your page, follow these steps:

1. Go to your Facebook page and click on the **About** tab.
2. Click on the **Edit** button next to the **Page Info** section.
3. Scroll down to the **Username** field and click on the **Create** button.
4. Enter the desired username and click **Save.**

Once you have saved your username, your Facebook URL will be updated to reflect the name of your page. You can share this URL with customers and promote it on your other social media platforms and online listings to drive traffic to your Facebook page and increase engagement with your brand. A simple method for this is to simply direct people to find you on Facebook using the @ symbol. For example, my Facebook page is @jeanleepublishing. Entering @jeanleepublishing into the Facebook search bar will take you directly to my page.

The **About** section of your Facebook page has two description fields: a **Short Description** and a **Long Description**. The *Short*

Description is a brief overview of your business, while the *Long Description* provides more detailed information.

- Use the *Short Description* to provide a brief overview of your Etsy shop, such as the exact types of products you offer, your target audience, and what your niche or theme is. Keep it concise and to the point, using keywords that accurately describe your business. Using the digital children's coloring book example, a good description might be, *Welcome to the Facebook page for our Etsy shop! We offer a wide selection of digital downloads featuring fun and creative coloring book pages for children to enjoy. Our digital downloads make it easy and convenient for you to print and share with your little ones. Join our coloring community today and spark your child's creativity with our unique designs!*

- Use the *Long Description* to provide more detailed information about your business, such as your shop's history, goals, and unique selling points. This is a good place to share your Etsy journey, explain why you started your business, and what your long-term goals are. For example, *Welcome to the Facebook page for our Etsy shop! We specialize in creating fun and imaginative coloring book pages for children that are designed to spark their creativity and inspire their imaginations. Our digital downloads offer a convenient and easy way to access our unique designs, which can be printed and shared with your little ones anytime, anywhere. Our collection features a wide range of themes, including animals, nature, holidays, and more, so you're sure to find something your child will love. At our shop, we're committed to providing high-quality products and exceptional customer service. We believe that coloring is not only a fun and entertaining activity for kids, but also a great way to improve fine motor skills, hand-eye coordination, and concentration. We're passionate about what we do and are proud to be a part of a community that encourages creativity and imagination in children. Join our coloring community today and discover the joy and benefits of coloring with our unique and exciting designs!*

In addition to filling out the *About* section of your Facebook business page with information about your Etsy shop, you can also use the **General Information** field to share links to your other social media accounts.

To **add links to your other social media accounts** (which we will discuss more later in this chapter), follow these steps:

1. Go to your Facebook page and click on the **About** tab.
2. Click on the **Edit** button next to the **Page Info** section.
3. Scroll down to the **General Information** field and click on the **Add a Website** button.

4. Enter the URL of your social media account and click **Save.**

5. Repeat the process until you have added links to all of your pages.

You can add links to as many social media accounts as you like, including Instagram, Twitter, Pinterest, YouTube, LinkedIn, and TikTok. It's important to note that you should **put the address to your Etsy shop in the main Website field**, as your primary goal is to drive traffic to your Etsy listings.

One way to make it easy for users to shop your Etsy listings from your Facebook page is to add a **Shop Now** tab with a call-to-action (CTA) button. This will create a direct link to your Etsy shop, allowing users to easily browse and purchase your products.

To **add a Shop Now tab to your Facebook business page**, follow these steps:

1. Go to your Facebook page and click on the **More** tab at the top of the page.

2. Select **Manage Tabs** from the drop-down menu.

3. Scroll down to the **Add a Tab** section and click on the **Add a Button** icon.

4. From the list of options, select **Shop Now** as the type of CTA button you want to add.

5. Enter the URL of your Etsy shop in the **Webpage Link** field and click **Save.**

The *Shop Now* tab and CTA button will now appear on your Facebook business page, allowing users to easily access your Etsy listings and make purchases. You can customize the text and appearance of the CTA button to match your branding and create a cohesive look and feel for your page. And you can change these settings at any time.

The **Settings** tab on your Facebook page allows you to control how users can interact with you and your page. This is important if you want to limit the types of interactions you receive, such as comments and messages. I don't allow people to message me on Facebook as I want to direct them to either my Etsy or Amazon shops as I don't sell outside of those platforms. However, the choice of whether or not to allow messages is completely up to you.

To **access the Settings tab**, follow these steps:

1. Go to your Facebook page and click on the **Settings** tab at the top of the page.
2. From the left-hand menu, select **Messages** to manage your messaging preferences.
3. Under the **General** section, you can choose to allow or block users from messaging you and whether or not you want to receive notifications when you receive a new message.

4. You can also choose to allow or block users from posting on your page and whether or not you want to receive notifications when you receive a new post.

5. Scroll down to the **Blocking** section to block specific users or groups from interacting with your page.

Once you have set up your Facebook business page, you need to start building your audience by getting people to "like" your page. Facebook will prompt you to invite friends and family from your personal account to "like" your new page and most of the people you are connected with will give your page a follow. However, remember that you can't expect your friends and family to buy from you. To build a business, you need to reach beyond your immediate circle.

While creating a Facebook business page is free, there are some paid options that Facebook offers to help grow your business. Facebook Ads allow you to target specific groups of people who may be interested in your products and encourage them to "like" your page to click through to your Etsy shop.

To create a Facebook ad:

1. Go to your Facebook business page and click on the **Create** button at the top of the page.

2. From the drop-down menu, select **Ad** to create a new ad campaign.

3. **Choose your ad objective.** Facebook offers a range of ad objectives to choose from, including "Website Visits," "Conversions," "Product Catalog Sales," and more. I recommend "Website Visits" because, after all, the goal is to bring customers to your Etsy shop.

4. **Set up your targeting options.** Facebook allows you to target specific groups of people based on demographics, interests, behaviors, and more. Use the targeting options to narrow down your audience to the people most likely to be interested in your products. You can do this by typing in keywords that relate to your products.

5. **Select your ad placements.** You can choose to show your ad on Facebook, Instagram, or both, as well as on other platforms such as "Audience Network" and "Marketplace." I choose all options so that my ad has the widest reach.

6. **Set your budget and schedule.** Decide how much you want to spend on your ad campaign and over what period. You can choose to run your ad continuously or set specific start and end dates. I usually start with $5 a day to test the ad.

7. **Create your ad.** Use the ad creation tools to design your ad, including the ad format, images, text, and call-to-action (CTA) button. You can choose from a variety of ad formats, including single images, carousels, and videos. I recommend adding a few of your best-selling product photos.

8. **Review and submit your ad.** Once you have finished creating your ad, review all the details to make sure everything is correct. When you are ready, click **Submit** to create your ad campaign.

The **Boost Post** feature on Facebook is a paid advertising tool that allows you to promote a specific post from your Facebook business page to a larger audience. This is an easier method than creating an ad from scratch.

To **boost a post from your Facebook business page**, follow these steps:

1. Go to your Facebook business page and find the post that you want to promote.
2. Click on the **Boost Post** button below the post.
3. **Select your target audience.** You can choose to show your boosted post to people who already like your page, to a specific group of people based on demographics and interests, or to a custom audience that you define. I usually choose to have the post shown to people who "like" my page and their friends and family. This way the people they are connected to will see that their friend or family member "likes" my business, which can encourage them to check it out.

4. **Set your budget and duration**. Decide how much you want to spend on your boosted post and over what period. You can choose to boost your post for as little as $1 per day or as much as you want. I like to choose a seven-day option with a budget of no more than $35 ($5 per day) to test how the ad performs.

5. **Review and boost your post.** Once you have finished setting up your boosted post, review all the details to make sure everything is correct. When you are ready, click **Boost** to promote your post.

So, you have set up a Facebook page for your business and have started getting people to "like" it. Now you need to commit to posting regular content on your page to keep your followers engaged. Creating engagement isn't just about seeing followers see your posts but also interacting with them by clicking the "thumbs up" button, leaving comments, or sharing your posts on their Facebook feeds to get their friends and family to like your page, too.

I always share my newest listings directly to my Facebook page, which Etsy makes easy to do. To **share an Etsy listing on your Facebook page**, follow these steps:

1. Go to your Etsy shop and find the listing that you want to share.

2. Click on the **Share** button below the listing.

3. Select **Facebook** from the drop-down menu.

4. A pop-up window will appear, asking you to log in to your Facebook account. Enter your login credentials and click **Log In.**

5. A new window will appear, allowing you to customize the message that will be posted to your Facebook page along with the listing. You can add a message or simply leave the default message.

6. When you are ready, click **Post to Facebook** to share the listing on your Facebook page.

In addition to promoting your listings on Facebook, try to engage with your followers. You can do this by posting updates about new product launches, your best-selling products for a particular week or month, or other relevant information such as deadlines for holiday orders. Creating polls about new product ideas is another easy way to create engagement as people are more likely to interact with a call-to-action post than just a standard post. Note that when people engage with your Facebook posts, Facebook may show the engagement in that person's feed so that their friends can see it. And those friends, seeing that they know someone who follows your page, may decide to follow your page, too.

It's important to keep your posts positive and avoid posting about controversial or offensive topics. In other words, unless you are selling religious or political-themed products, avoid those two topics. The goal of your business page is to attract customers and make money. Posting about sensitive subjects can turn people away. Make sure to stick to topics related to your business or that are lighthearted and save the personal commentary for your personal account.

However, that's not to say you can't have non-business content on your Facebook business page. Sharing a picture of your lunch while you take a break from designing or posting a meme related to your niche can often bring more engagement than posting a new listing. A picture of your pet, a funny quote, or simply wishing your customers a "happy-whatever-holiday-it-is" can go a long way toward building rapport with your followers. And the more rapport you have with your followers, the more likely they are to turn into customers.

Facebook Groups: As your business grows, you may decide to create a special Facebook group just for your Etsy shop customers. I have a Facebook group for my Etsy sticker shop that lets me connect with my best customers. They help me narrow down new sticker designs, and I reward their loyalty with special discount codes.

To **start a Facebook group:**

1. Log into Facebook and navigate to your business page.

2. In the top right corner of your page, click the **Create Group** button.

3. Select either **Close** (a private group that only members can access), **Secret** (an even more private group that only members can see and that doesn't appear in search results), or **Public** (a group that anyone can see and join). I have my group set to private so that Facebook users can see it but only members can see what is being posted. Since I post exclusive discount codes in the group, I want to make sure only members can see those posts.

4. Choose a **name and description** that accurately represents your business and the purpose of the group. I recommend selecting a name that matches up with your Etsy shop. My Etsy sticker shop is "Jean Lee Publishing," and my Facebook group is "Jean Lee's Sticker Club."

5. You can **invite members** by searching for Facebook users, adding email addresses, or inviting members from your business page.

6. You can **customize group settings** such as who can post and comment, who can see the group, and who can be added as a member.

7. When you're ready, click the **Create** button to launch your group. You can start posting updates and engaging with members right away.

It's hard to start a group until you have people following your Facebook page. And having a group isn't a necessity for any business. As your business grows and you build up a loyal customer base, it may be something to consider, especially if you are in a niche where you have the potential for repeat customers. For instance, most people will only buy wedding invitations once. But parents will buy digital coloring pages again and again for their children. A group to showcase all of your coloring pages is more logical than a group for wedding invitations.

Twitter: Like Facebook, Twitter is another free social media platform that you can use to promote your Etsy shop. With Twitter, you can share short updates, called "tweets," with your followers and engage with them through **@replies** and **#hashtags.**

If you don't already have a Twitter account, you can create one for free at Twitter.com. Note that if you have an existing personal Twitter account that you are active on, you may want to consider creating a separate account for your Etsy business to keep your personal and professional lives separate. You can create multiple Twitter accounts; you just need to use separate email addresses. You can create email addresses for free using Google at https://accounts.google.com/signup.

Remember as you are creating social media pages for your Etsy shop to use the same handle for your Twitter account as you have for your Etsy shop and Facebook page to create a consistent online presence for your business. This will make it easier for people to find and follow you across different platforms and helps in building your brand.

Twitter limits their "tweets" to 280 characters or less. Etsy makes it easy to share your listings on Twitter by including a share button in all active listings. To use the Twitter share button, simply click on it within a listing, and a new window will open on Twitter with the title of your listing and the direct link to it already populated. You can send the "tweet" as is or customize the message as well as add hashtags.

Hashtags (marked as such with the # sign) are a way to categorize and organize content on social media platforms, especially on Twitter. In fact, I find that hashtags are more useful on Twitter than on any other platform as users are more accustomed to using them there than on other sites. Twitter users can follow their favorite hashtags to keep up with the posts they are most interested in seeing.

Adding hashtags to your "tweets" is an easy way to increase the chance of your posts being found by interested shoppers. By adding relevant hashtags to your tweets, you are making it easier for people to discover your Etsy business and perhaps buy your items.

For example, let's use our children's coloring book digital download as an example. When you click on the Twitter icon in the listing, your title and the link to the listing will automatically populate to Twitter. If there is room to add more text, you can add hashtags such as #etsy, #etsyshop, #coloringbooks, and #printables. If the coloring book is for a specific occasion or holiday, such as Christmas or summer vacation, add hashtags to represent those events. These hashtags will help your tweet show up in searches for these topics, meaning they will show up for Twitter users following those hashtags.

It's important not to overuse hashtags or use ones that are not relevant to your business. This can make your tweets seem spammy and could turn people off. Instead, choose around five relevant hashtags that accurately describe your business and the products you are selling. While the bridal category is huge on Etsy, don't use the hashtag #bridal in your listings if you sell children's coloring books.

As with sharing your Facebook page with customers, you also want to share your Twitter handle, both online and offline, to encourage them to follow you on the platform. Including your Twitter handle in your other social media profiles and on any other promotional materials will help your customers find you.

One way to build up your followers on Twitter is to follow other users and engage with their content. Some users follow everyone who follows them, which can help increase your follower count. You can also use Twitter's @reply and retweet features to engage with other users and share their content with your followers. This can help build relationships and expose your content to a wider audience.

Because digital downloads are such a competitive category on Etsy, I recommend NOT following other digital creators on Etsy. Instead, look for Etsy shops that sell physical products such as crafts and antiques. Etsy sellers like to support each other as long as they aren't competing for the same group of customers.

Just like on Facebook, you can use Twitter to send and receive messages from other users. On Twitter, these messages are called **Direct Messages,** or **DMs** for short. You can send DMs to any user who is following you, and you can also receive DMs from users who you follow. Or you can block messaging.

In addition to messaging, Twitter also allows you to create **Lists** to group users you follow into categories. Lists are a useful way to organize and keep track of the accounts you follow, and they can also be used to create customized feeds of tweets from specific users. For example, you might create a list of "customers," "Etsy shops," "digital products," or "printables" to help you stay organized and focused on the content that is most relevant to your business.

Instagram: Like Facebook, Instagram is a social media platform that allows users to share photos and videos and engage with their followers. There are several features on Instagram that you can use to share your content about your Etsy shop:

- **Instagram Posts:** *Instagram Posts* are static photos that you share on your profile. They are visible to all your followers and remain on your profile indefinitely unless you delete them. *Instagram Posts* are an easy way to share the images of your products, which is easy to do by simply reposting the same images to Instagram that you use in your Etsy listings.

- **Instagram Stories:** *Instagram Stories* are photos or videos that you share on your profile that disappear after 24 hours. *Instagram Stories* are a good way to share behind-the-scenes glimpses of your business, sneak peeks of new products, or more personal content that you may want to share with your followers but that doesn't need to remain on your profile indefinitely. For example, while I want pictures of my products to always appear on my profile page, I don't need to permanently save a short video of me visiting a local attraction. Note that you can also share your static posts to your stories to make sure those posts get maximum exposure.

- **Instagram Reels:** *Instagram Reels* allows users to create and share short video clips of up to one minute and thirty seconds that can be edited with music, effects, and custom text. *Instagram Reels* is a good way to create and share fun content that highlights your products. As with static posts, you can also share *Instagram Reels* to your *Instagram Stories.*

PRO TIP: Because Facebook owns Instagram, you can connect your accounts so that your Instagram posts will automatically share to your Facebook business page. This is a great time saver as you don't have to create two different posts for each site.

In addition to using Instagram to promote your Etsy listings, you can also use the platform to connect with your customers on a more personal level by sharing photos that may not always relate directly to your business. For example, you can post photos of your office, designs you are working on, and other behind-the-scenes glimpses of your shop. You can also share photos of your pets, meals, or other fun snapshots to give your followers a more personal look at your life. Remember, however, that you are using Instagram to promote your Etsy shop. Just as with your other social media business pages, you should avoid sharing controversial or offensive content.

Just as you use hashtags on Twitter, they are also a useful tool on Instagram. Here are a few tips for using hashtags effectively on Instagram to promote your Etsy shop:

1. **Use relevant hashtags:** Make sure to use hashtags that are relevant to your business and the content you are sharing. This will help ensure that your posts are seen by users who are interested in what you are selling. As an Etsy digital shop, stick to hashtags related to the niche and products you are selling. Many people will use hashtags that have nothing to do with their Etsy shop to be seen by more users. But this can backfire if those users are annoyed seeing your content in their feed and react negatively by leaving mean comments under your posts.

2. **Use a mix of popular and niche hashtags:** Using popular hashtags can help increase the visibility of your content but using too many popular hashtags can make it harder for your content to stand out. Consider using a mix of hashtags to balance visibility and relevance. For example, you want to use the hashtags #etsy and #etsyshop in most of your Instagram posts. But also add hashtags of the theme of the products you are posting about. If you are sharing listings about custom Father's Day card downloads, use hashtags such as #dad, #fathersday, and #giftsfordad to reach people who follow those specific tags.

3. **Don't overdo it:** Using too many hashtags can make your content look spammy and may turn off some users. Aim to use around five hashtags per post to strike a good balance between visibility and relevance. I have a list of hashtags in the notes section of my smartphone that I can copy, paste, and edit when I am creating a new post.

Narrowing down the hashtags you want to include can be a challenge as there are so many potential options. For instance, if you are selling personalized Christmas cards, you could choose from numerous hashtags, including:

- #etsy
- #etsyshop
- #christmas
- #etsychristmasshop
- #christmascards
- #personlizedcards
- #customcards
- #personazliedgifts
- #personalizedcards
- #christmasgifts
- #holidaygifts
- #giftsforher
- #giftsforhim

- #giftsformom
- #giftsfordad
- #cards

Utilizing a site such as EtsyCheck or eRank can help you find the best hashtags to use. I like to use a mix of popular and more niche hashtags to reach the widest audience possible. I use EtsyCheck to find keywords for my listings and hashtags for my social media.

Linking Your Shop: You cannot add a live link to your Etsy shop in static Instagram posts, meaning if you add your Etsy shop's URL, it won't be clickable for users. However, Instagram allows you to include one live clickable website link in your profile, which you can use to link to your Etsy shop.

To drive traffic to your Etsy listings on Instagram in static posts, you can share photos and include a message in the caption that directs your followers to your profile page, where they can find an active link to your Etsy shop. For example, you can write "Brand new coloring book printables are now available in our Etsy shop! Follow the link in our profile @yourinstagramaccount to shop now!"

By including the @ symbol and your Instagram handle, you will create a clickable link that will take users to your profile page, where they can click on the link to your Etsy shop and browse your listings. You can also create a live clickable link in your Instagram stories by using the **Link** option.

If you want to share multiple links on Instagram, you will need to use a service like **Linktr.ee** to create a landing page that allows you to list all your links in one place. When you create a *Linktr.ee* page, you can add as many links as you like, and users will be able to access them all by clicking on the main *Linktr.ee* link in your Instagram profile. To see an example, visit my *Linktr.ee* page at **linktr.ee/anneckhart.**

As with Twitter, you'll want to connect with other Etsy sellers on Instagram. However, try to avoid other digital product shops as the market is too competitive and you don't want to create a target on your shop from other shop owners. Instead, search out the hashtags #etsyshop and #etsyseller to find accounts that are selling other Etsy products such as vintage collectibles and crafts.

Pinterest: Pinterest is a social media platform that allows users to share and discover ideas and inspiration by "pinning" images and videos to virtual boards. Etsy allows users to create "boards" where they "pin" posts, similar to how one uses a bulletin board. Users create different "boards" for different categories and niches.

As with Facebook and Twitter, Etsy includes a share button in all active listings that makes it easy to share your listings on Pinterest. You can share your Etsy listings on specific boards that you have created that relate to your category and various niches such as a "Printables for Kids" board or a "Custom Wedding Invitations" board. I recommend starting a board that coincides with every one of your shop's sections.

As with the other social media platforms, you can use hashtags to make it easier for people to discover your Pinterest boards, although hashtags aren't used as much on Pinterest as they are on other sites. Pinterest is much more of a visual platform, so make sure the pictures you share are the best quality you have.

Finding content on Pinterest that coordinates with your products and re-pinning those posts as well as following their creators is another way to connect with not only other accounts but also the people who follow those accounts. However, as we've already discussed, avoid other digital product sellers as you don't want to create unnecessary competition. Rather, search for content that relates to your niche. For instance, if you sell wedding printables, follow boards about wedding planning. If you sell educational products, follow boards about teaching and homeschooling.

If you do become active on Pinterest, be sure to share your Pinterest account with your customers and followers on other social media platforms and any promotional materials. You can easily add your Pinterest account to the links section of your Facebook business page.

TikTok: TikTok is a social media platform that allows users to create and share short videos, also referred to as "short-form content."

TikTok began with a younger demographic but is slowly growing with users of all ages. On TikTok, users can create short videos (up to three minutes) that can be edited with music, effects, and other creative tools. From comedy skits and dances to personal stories and small business, there are TikTok videos for every interest.

Since TikTok relies on short-form videos, it can be challenging to come up with content related to a digital product business. After all, printables aren't quite as engaging as vintage toys, handmade crafts, or even print-on-demand clothing. However, since most digital products can easily be printed out, you can showcase your printables in action by writing or coloring them.

There are two types of TikTok accounts available: personal and business. A **TikTok personal account** is an account that is for personal use. Most personal accounts aren't interested in growing a large following but are on TikTok just for fun.

A **TikTok business account**, however, is an account that is specifically designed for businesses to use on the platform. Business accounts on TikTok have access to features and tools that are not available to personal accounts, such as analytics, advertising, and the ability to create and manage ads.

The biggest benefit of a TikTok business account is that you can put a clickable URL in your profile. I have my Linktr.ee link in my TikTok business account profile, which will take people to a static page with all of my business links, including a link to my Etsy shop. Personal TikTok accounts can't put a clickable link in their profiles. And as with all social media platforms, your main goal should be driving traffic to your Etsy shop, which is much easier to do with a live link.

If you want to use TikTok to promote your Etsy business, you definitely want to create a TikTok business account. Note that you can create multiple TikTok pages within one account; if you already have a personal account, you can easily add a second business account. It's a simple process to switch back and forth between your multiple accounts without having to constantly log out and back in.

To create a TikTok business account for an Etsy shop, you will need to follow these steps:

1. **Download the TikTok app** on your phone or tablet.
2. Open the app and tap on the **Me** icon in the bottom right corner.
3. Tap on the **three dots** in the top right corner and select **Manage account**.
4. Tap on **Switch to Professional Account**.
5. Select **Business** as the account type.

6. Follow the prompts to complete the account setup process, including adding your business name, contact information, and any other required information.

Once your account is set up, you can start creating and sharing content to promote your Etsy shop. Keep in mind that TikTok may require you to verify your business account before you can access all the features and tools available to business accounts. This may involve providing additional information or documentation to prove that you are the owner of the business.

There are several ways you can use TikTok to promote your Etsy business:

Create and share posts about your products: Use TikTok's creative tools and features, such as music, effects, and filters, to create short, entertaining videos that highlight your products creatively and engagingly. Print out your digital products and show yourself writing or coloring on them.

Participate in trends: TikTok is famous for trending dances, challenges, and filters. Participating in these is a fantastic way to create engagement. While the trends may not have anything to do with your business, because they are so popular, your posts are bound to get more views. A good rule of thumb is to post one business post for every three fun posts. Make sure to only participate in trends that are non-controversial and won't harm your business image.

Use relevant hashtags and tags: By including relevant hashtags and tags in your TikTok posts, you can make it easier for users to discover your content and interact with your account as well as hopefully visit your Etsy shop. However, as we've already discussed, unlike other Etsy shops, you don't want to use any hashtags relating to your business model. For example, you don't want to use the hashtags #digitalcreator, #printondemand, or #dropshipping. It is okay, however, to use the hashtags #etsy, #etsyshop, and #etsyseller. Add additional hashtags that relate directly to your niche and products such as #coloringpages or #weddingstationery.

You can also try searching for hashtags related to specific themes or categories, such as #weddings or #christams. Additionally, you can use TikTok's search function to discover more hashtags related to your specific niche. Searching for the hashtag #weddings will lead you to the trending bridal hashtags. And when you discover new hashtags, you will also find new targets to create products for.

As I mentioned in the Instagram section of this chapter, I keep a list of hashtags in the notes section of my phone that I just copy and paste into posts. TikTok allows you to write up to 2,200 characters in the caption of a post. However, it's worth noting that captions on TikTok are rarely read, as the main focus is on the video content and the related hashtags rather than the written text. A caption of around 100-200 characters is considered optimal for TikTok, as it allows for enough text to add context and engage with the audience, but still keeps the focus on the video. However, there are many times I only add hashtags with no other text.

Utilize TikTok's advertising features: TikTok's business accounts have access to advertising features that can help you reach a wider audience beyond those who follow your account and drive traffic to your Etsy shop. You can create and manage ads on TikTok to reach users who are interested in your products or related topics based on their activities on the app, which TikTok tracks. TikTok's advertising opportunities include:

- **In-feed ads:** These are native ads that appear in users' feeds, like sponsored posts on other social media platforms. They can be in the form of videos, photos, or carousels and can include a call-to-action button.
- **Brand takeover ads:** These are full-screen ads that appear when a user opens the app. They can be in the form of a video or image and are a great way to grab users' attention.
- **Branded hashtag challenge:** This feature allows businesses to create a hashtag challenge, which encourages users to create and share content using the designated hashtag.

- **Branded effects:** TikTok's AR effects allow businesses to create their own branded filters and lenses that users can use in their videos.
- **Branded hashtag stickers:** These are branded stickers that users can use in their videos and are associated with a specific hashtag.

To access TikTok's advertising platform, you will need to sign up for a **TikTok Ads account**. Here's how you can do that:

1. Go to the TikTok Ads website at **tiktok.com/business/ad-center**.
2. Click on the **Sign-Up** button in the top right corner of the page.
3. Fill in the required information to create a new account, including your name, email address, and password.

Once you have created your account, you can access TikTok's advertising platform by logging in to the TikTok Ads website and clicking on the **Create** button in the top right corner of the page. From there, you can choose the type of ad you want to create and follow the prompts to set up your campaign.

YouTube: Starting a YouTube channel can be a great way to promote digital products you sell on Etsy. Just as you print out and show your items in posts on Facebook, Twitter, Instagram,

Pinterest, and TikTok, you can also film videos of your products to share on YouTube.

Why start a YouTube channel to promote your digital products? For one, it's free and relatively easy to do. You don't even need a digital camera to film videos; I use my iPhone to film my YouTube videos. YouTube has over 2 billion active users and is the second-largest search engine in the world. By starting a channel, you can reach a larger audience and increase exposure for your products.

Like TikTok, YouTube allows you a way to showcase your products via videos but in a longer format. You can create tutorials on how to download, print, and use your products. And you can introduce new items as you release them. By including links to your Etsy store in your video descriptions or even within the videos themselves, you can drive traffic directly to your store and potentially increase sales.

Not sure how exactly YouTube works? Check out my book, *Beginner's Guide To Starting a YouTube Channel,* which is available on Amazon.

PRO TIP: An easy way to create multiple social media posts with one single clip is to film a 60-second TikTok video. Save that video and share it on Instagram as a Reel. The Reel will post to your Instagram feed; from there, share the Reel to your Instagram Stories. If your Instagram and Facebook pages are linked, the clip will also post to your Facebook page. And if you have a YouTube channel, you can share the clip as a Short. One 60-minute video will gain you maximum exposure across all of your social media platforms!

Etsy's Marketing Tools: While social media platforms such as Facebook, Instagram, Twitter, Pinterest, TikTok, and YouTube are all great ways to build your digital brand, Etsy itself offers several marketing tools to help sellers promote their products and reach new customers.

Some of the marketing tools available on Etsy include:

Shop Announcements: This feature allows you to create a message that will be displayed on your shop's homepage and in the emails you send to your customers. You can use this section to announce new product releases, highlight your best-selling products, share the story behind your shop, offer special promotions and discounts, and keep the customer informed of any changes or updates to your shop.

Etsy Ads: *Etsy Ads* allow you to create targeted ads that will be displayed to potential customers who are searching for products like yours on Etsy. To **create an ad for your shop on Etsy**, go to your **Seller Dashboard** and click on the **Marketing** tab. Click on **Etsy Ads**. Choose a daily budget anywhere from $1 to $100.

I recommend starting with $5 a day and letting the ad run for at least a week to see how it performs. If you are correctly utilizing

Etsy SEO and are using social media to promote your shop, you may find that Etsy Ads aren't worth the added expense. But the only way you can know for sure is to test them out.

Etsy Offsite Ads: As we've discussed, this feature allows you to place ads that will be displayed on other websites and platforms, such as Facebook, Instagram, Pinterest, and Google. For sellers with less than $10,000 in yearly sales, Etsy *Offsite Ads* are an optional program one needs to opt into. However, it is mandatory and automatic for shops that sell over $10,000 a year.

Remember that you only pay for an offsite ad if it leads to a sale. You do not pay if someone clicks on the ad but does not make a purchase. So, there is no risk to opting into these ads as you aren't going to lose money, but you will have the potential to make more.

You can end your *Offsite Ads* at any time unless you are automatically enrolled due to selling over $10,000 a year. There is no way to end or opt out of *Offsite Ads* for sellers who sell over $10,000. While this may seem unfair, to be honest, if you are selling over $10,000 a year on Etsy, *Offsite Ads* should be affordable for you. Again, you only pay if the click on an ad leads to a sale, meaning you aren't risking anything.

To access the **Offside Ads** section of your account, go to your **Seller Dashboard** and click on the **Settings** tab. Then click on **Offsite Ads.**

Sales & Discounts: You can create various sales and discounts for both new and returning customers. You will find the **Sales & Discounts** section under the **Marketing** tab in your Etsy dashboard.

You can offer a **percentage off** the purchase price for a specific product or the entire order. For example, you could offer a 10% discount on all Christmas digital products in your shop or offer a 20% discount on all orders over $50. Etsy automatically applies the discount for you, and the offer is shown in your listings, which can help draw customers in. For example, in my Etsy sticker shop, I frequently offer 30% off any three items. That 30% discount shows up under the price of all of my listings, which entices shoppers to click through to my shop to learn more about the sale. I find that when I run a sale, my orders increase, even if customers don't end up ordering enough to score the discount.

In contract to offering a percentage off, you can instead offer a **fixed amount off** the purchase price for a specific product or the entire order. For example, you could offer a $5 discount on all custom digital products in your shop or a $10 discount on orders over $100. I don't find this amount off option to be as effective as the percentage off option, but you should test it out to see which works best for your shop.

Sale events: You can create a sales event by offering a discount on a selection of your products for a limited time. Some of the offers you can send include:

- **Thank you:** Invite up to 200 recent customers back with a thank you offer by sending them an offer to show appreciation and encourage them to shop again. You can choose a discount amount of a percentage off or a fixed amount off.

- **Favorited item:** Turn favorites into orders by sending offers to anyone who favors one of your items. You can choose a discount percentage or a fixed amount off. Note that there is no minimum order option for the *favorited item* offers; it applies to the single item that someone has put into their cart.

- **Abandoned cart:** Remind shoppers to check out by sending an offer when someone leaves an item from your shop in their cart. As with *favorited items*, you can choose a discount percentage or a fixed amount off; and there is no minimum order amount as the offer applies to a single item that someone has put into their cart.

- **Run a sale:** Set lower prices for your whole shop or select categories. Many professional Etsy sellers will tell you that you should always be running sales and that your sales should be short-term for no longer than 48 hours. This is because Etsy will show shoppers a countdown clock of the remaining time in a sale, which can create a sense of urgency. These sellers typically run the same sale every two days.

PRO TIP: Again, be careful with offering any discount or exclusive offer. The truth is that most Etsy sellers raise their prices over what the market rate is so that they can always have their items "on sale." And they often run short-term sales of 48 hours or less so that Etsy will show customers a count-down clock to encourage them to shop before the sale ends. Is it frustrating to have to play this "sale" game to get orders? Yes. But it is a fact of the retail industry. People buy more items when they are on sale. Making sure you know your numbers so you can play the discount game will help you sell more items.

Before offering any type of discount, use an Etsy fee calculator to figure out your costs. You may find you need to raise your prices to justify running a "sale." There are many free Etsy fee calculators available online. My personal favorite is https://omniprofitcalculator.com/etsy-fee-calculator/.

Create a promo code: Etsy allows shops to create a custom code to send to customers directly. You will need to enter a code name, a description of the offer, and the discount amount. You can also choose to set an expiration date and a minimum purchase amount. You can manually end your coupon codes at any time.

Etsy does not distribute these coupon codes; that is something you need to do. If you have a mailing list or Facebook group, you can share these special promo codes with those customers. I have a Facebook group specifically for my Etsy sticker shop and frequently create special promo codes just for members.

Product reviews: If you are struggling to grow your Etsy business, you might consider reaching out to social media content creators to see if they will feature your products in a YouTube video, TikTok, or Instagram post. Note that if the person has a large following that they will charge for such a service, and often this cost is too much for a beginning shop owner to afford. However, smaller creators who are trying to get their platforms off the ground are usually open to receiving free items in exchange for honest reviews.

Collaboration: Another way to market your products is to collaborate with other Etsy shop owners to exchange products where you will both do reviews of the other's items in a video or social media post. Avoid collaborating with digital shops that sell in the same category you do as you will only be creating competition. Rather, look for shops that sell complimentary products. If you sell custom wedding invitations, for example, you might look for a shop that makes wedding favors.

Blog/Website: Creating a blog or dedicated website can be a great way to establish your brand. By regularly updating your site with posts about new products, you can keep visitors engaged and interested. This can be especially valuable if you plan to make selling digital products your primary source of income and if you plan to extend your business on sites other than Etsy.

However, if your Etsy shop is only a hobby or part-time job, or if you don't want to sell anywhere other than Etsy, you don't need to create a dedicated website or blog. Instead, you can focus on promoting your products on Etsy directly as well as on the social media platforms we've already covered.

If you do decide to create a website, you should consider whether you have the time and resources to maintain it regularly. Some things to consider when deciding whether to create a website include:

- Do you plan to author lengthy articles discussing the items you sell? Blogs are often seen as a research source on various topics. If you plan to only post new products and not offer any other information besides that, a website isn't worth your time.
- Are you looking to use your site not just as a sales channel but also as a teaching tool? For example, if you sell

educational downloads, do you want to expand into articles targeted toward parents and teachers?

- Do you want to sell products only through Etsy or do you plan to eventually expand to selling on other platforms? If you do want to eventually grow beyond Etsy, then a website could serve as a landing page for all of your links.

- Do you want to explore affiliate advertising or sell advertising on your site to earn extra money? Google AdSense and Amazon Associates are just two of the programs that allow you to earn money by placing links on your blog.

If you answered "yes" to any of the above questions, then you may want to consider starting a website. However, you will need to decide whether to go with a free blogging platform or a paid website. If you decide to go the paid route, you can invest in a sophisticated system or choose a simple, low-cost one.

Yes, there are lots of decisions to make when deciding whether or not to start a website!

There are several free blogging platforms available, such as **Blogger** and **WordPress**, that you can use to create a blog for your Etsy shop. It's worth noting that Blogger is owned by Google, which means that you can apply for a Google AdSense account and place ads on your blog to generate additional revenue. In addition to driving traffic to your Etsy listings and increasing sales, a blog can be a useful way to monetize your online presence.

If you decide to create a paid website for your Etsy shop, it's important to do your research and choose a platform that meets your needs. Your Etsy shop should be the focus of your brand, with your blog or website serving as an additional tool to drive traffic to your listings. There are many low-cost website options available, such as **GoDaddy.com** and **Wix.com**, which offer not only URL registrations but also inexpensive hosting and simple website-building tools. Keep in mind that your goal is to drive traffic to your Etsy listings and increase sales, so choose a website platform that will help you achieve this.

If you expand the sale of your products on multiple websites in addition to Etsy, a blog or website can be a great place to provide links to those other platforms. A website can also help to establish your business as legitimate and build trust with potential customers, making them more likely to purchase from you than other sellers.

It's important to remember that maintaining your blog or website is just as important as creating it. In addition to posting regular updates, you should also make an effort to respond to any comments from visitors and ensure that all links are active and up to date.

Because I use the pen name Jean Lee for both my Etsy shop and the stationery products I sell on Amazon, I have a website at www.JeanLeePublishing.com that I use through GoDaddy that serves as a landing page for both platforms. When you register a URL with GoDaddy, they will offer you add-on options such as a website. This is the option I use for my Jean Lee site as it is inexpensive and easy to maintain.

Domain Name: If you are selling a large number of items on Etsy and plan to grow it to be your full-time job, you may want to consider registering for a **domain name,** which is a personal website address closely tied to your Etsy shop name. This can make it easier for customers to find and remember your website, as well as give you a professional online presence.

You can purchase domain names through websites like **GoDaddy.com** and link them to your Etsy shop and other online platforms. For example, I have the domain **AnnEckhart.com** that directs users directly to my Amazon Storefront where all my books are listed. And **JeanLeePublishing.com** takes users to a website that directs them to my Etsy shop or my Amazon page for my stationery brand, both of which I have under the same pen name.

When thinking about registering for a domain name, it's important to consider where you want the URL to direct users. Do you want people to go to your blog first, or do you want them to always go directly to your Etsy shop? It's important to remember that your blog or website should *complement* your Etsy shop, rather than serve as a replacement for it. So, unless you are selling products on multiple websites the way I am, you want your URL to point to Etsy.

If you are using a free blog on a platform like Blogger, you may want to choose a domain name that directs people directly to your Etsy shop, such as "MyStore.com", and keep the URL provided by Blogger for your blog as-is. Alternatively, you could choose a different domain name specifically for your blog, such as "MyEtsyShopBlog.com". The key is to choose a URL that makes sense for your business and helps to drive traffic to your Etsy shop.

In my opinion, it's important to have a personalized URL address that points directly to your Etsy shop, as your primary focus should always be on driving sales through Etsy. Your website should work to direct traffic to your Etsy listings, rather than intercept it. If you grow beyond Etsy, you can easily change your URL address to point to a different site.

Mailing List: Creating a strong digital product brand can lead to repeat customers who keep coming back to your store because they love your items. To keep these loyal customers informed and engaged, you may want to consider setting up a mailing list for you to send out newsletters. You can use newsletters to stay in touch with your customers by providing them with updates about your business, such as new product releases, exclusive offers, and other important news. You can also offer giveaways and other special deals only available to subscribers such as free downloads.

Some popular mailing list services include:

- AWeber
- Campaign Monitor
- Constant Contact
- Drip
- GetResponse
- Mailchimp

These services provide tools for creating and managing email campaigns, including email design templates, subscriber lists, analytics, and automation features. Many also offer integrations with other marketing and sales tools, such as e-commerce platforms and CRM software. Most offer their services for free until you hit a certain number of subscribers, after which you will need to pay.

PRO TIP: If you do start to collect email addresses for a mailing list, make sure you keep a file of those addresses on your computer system or backup hard drive, not only on the mailing list server. If you decide to stop using their mailing service, you will lose access to those emails. Always make sure you have a backup so you can start a new list with another service if you decide to.

Note that many blogs and website platforms also have a built-in mailing list feature. For example, I have my JeanLeePublishing.com, which is through GoDaddy, which has a feature where visitors can enter their email addresses to join my mailing list. I can use GoDaddy's newsletter feature or transfer the email addresses to another platform.

Remember to only send emails to individuals who have specifically opted in to receive them so that you comply with anti-spam laws and avoid annoying or alienating your customers. Send newsletters sparingly, no more than once a week. And only send newsletters when you have interesting and valuable content to share. It's better to send a monthly newsletter that is jam-packed with good content than it is to send weekly newsletters with little value.

Putting It All Together: If you're feeling overwhelmed by all the different social networking sites and techniques, take a deep breath and remember to take things one step at a time. Start with Facebook, as it is the easiest and most effective. Then expand to Twitter, Pinterest, and Instagram, as you can stick to static posts on all of them. If you feel comfortable adding videos, you can expand to TikTok and YouTube. Or just choose one to focus on, the one you most enjoy. Some Etsy shops only use Facebook, while others are solely focused on TikTok.

When you have an Etsy digital product shop, your primary focus should be developing new products, creating listings, answering customer questions, and processing orders. Etsy SEO, along with a good title, photos, and description are essential in creating an Etsy listing that will result in shoppers finding your products. Think of social media as a bonus step in that listing creation process.

To promote your listings on social media, remember that you can use the "share" buttons provided by Etsy in every active listing. Simply click on the buttons for Facebook, Twitter, and Pinterest to share your listings on these platforms. As we've discussed, hashtags are incredibly useful to increase the visibility of your social media posts. Once you have connected your Etsy account to your social media networks, you can easily share your listings with just a few clicks and add a handful of relevant hashtags.

To avoid overwhelming your followers on Facebook with multiple listings at once, I recommend spreading your posts out. You can schedule posts on Facebook to spread them out over the day. On Twitter and Pinterest, it is generally okay to share posts one after the other as the feeds on both platforms move much faster than on Facebook.

To promote your business on Instagram, it is important to post regularly and engage with other users. Try to post at least once a day You can share photos of your office, new inventory, or even personal moments to give your followers a behind-the-scenes look at your business. Don't forget to include three to five hashtags with each post to make it easier for users to find you. Try adding videos to Instagram through Reels and Stories. Once you are comfortable creating videos, consider expanding to TikTok and even YouTube.

If you have the time and resources to create and maintain a website, this can be a great way to promote your digital brand. However, remember that a website will require additional work and resources, so it's important to make sure it is worth the investment. I don't recommend a website unless you expand to selling on sites other than Etsy. And even then you want to manage your time effectively and prioritize your efforts so that you can get the most benefit from your efforts.

Remember that your number one goal with your business is to make money. Your priority should always be developing new products, creating new listings, and maximizing Etsy SEO. You may find that you do enough on Etsy alone to make sales!

CHAPTER NINE: ETSY ACCOUNTING MADE EASY

Let's be real: Making money is fun, but dealing with taxes and bookkeeping is not. However, when you're running your own business, keeping track of your finances is essential. You have to know your numbers to make sure you're turning a profit, and you must report your earnings to the government come tax time.

Luckily, the bookkeeping tasks for a digital product business are pretty straightforward. There's no inventory to track, no shipping supplies to buy, and not much driving around to log mileage for. All of your expenses are online, which makes tracking your receipts easy.

Of course, you should always consult with a certified public accountant (CPA) to discuss the tax laws that apply to your business. You can even hire a CPA to file your taxes. However, you still need to keep track of things on your end to ensure you are making more money than you are spending and to accurately provide a CPA with your information come tax time.

Fortunately, Etsy provides sellers with a lot of financial information to help them keep track of your numbers. Specifically, Etsy breaks down your expenses, including the fees you paid to them and the cost of any ads or promotions you ran on their platform. They automatically deduct these expenses for you, depositing the remaining funds in your account as your net profit.

All this financial information is stored and updated in real time in your account. From your **Shop Manager** dashboard, click on **Finances** to access the following:

Payment Account: The *Payment Account* section is where you can manage your payment and deposit information. To receive payment for the items you sell, you must link your bank account to Etsy. You have the option to choose your preferred deposit schedule from daily, weekly, every other week, or monthly transfers. I choose weekly payouts so that I can count on a weekly "paycheck."

Monthly Statements: The *Monthly Statements* section is, in my opinion, the most important part of the *Finances* area. Here you can access information about your sales, fees, marketing expenses, shipping costs, and net profit. You can view your monthly statements dating back to the beginning of your selling account or narrow down the time frame to however you choose.

Regularly monitoring your net profit will give you an idea of whether you are making money or incurring a loss. Remember to keep in mind that the net profit displayed by Etsy does not include your offline expenses, such as your internet costs, cell phone fees, and graphics subscriptions.

QuickBooks for Etsy: For a fee, you can sync your Etsy seller account with *Intuit QuickBooks* to track your sales, expenses, and tax deductions.

TurboTax for Etsy: For a fee, you can sync your Etsy seller account with *TurboTax*, which will organize your account for taxes.

Legal & Tax Information: The *Legal & Tax Information* section is where you will enter all the necessary legal information for your shop. It is in this section that you will be able to download your 1099 form at the end of the year, which is required for tax filing purposes. If you sell more than $600 within the year, Etsy will generate a 1099 tax form for you. Note that even if you are not issued a tax form, you still must report all income to the IRS.

Fees: All selling platforms charge their sellers fees, and Etsy is no exception. As we've already discussed, the fees Etsy charges cover the costs of operating the platform and providing services to its users. These fees include a **listing fee**, a **transaction fee**, and a **payment processing fee.**

To recap from earlier in this book, Etsy charges a **listing fee** whenever a seller creates a new listing. This fee is currently $0.20 per listing and is charged at the time the listing is created. Listings are active for four months and can be renewed by the seller at the end of that period for an additional $0.20. That means you can list one item for a year for only $.80.

Etsy also charges a **transaction fee** whenever an item sells. This fee is currently 5% of the item's sale price, plus any shipping and gift wrap charges. The transaction fee is charged at the time the sale is made. As a digital product seller, you obviously won't have to worry about shipping or gift-wrapping costs.

Finally, Etsy charges a **payment processing fee** whenever they process a sale. This fee varies depending on the payment method used but is typically around 3% of the total transaction amount plus a fixed fee. The payment processing fee is deducted from the seller's account at the time the payment is processed.

Expenses: All businesses can claim business-related expenses as deductions on their taxes. With an Etsy digital product shop, the fees you will need to track are:

- **Fees:** The fees charged by Etsy are automatically deducted from your account before your net profit is disbursed to you. If the fees are not specified on the tax form issued by Etsy, then you shouldn't need to report them during tax season. However, check with your CPA or tax preparer to be sure you are following the current tax laws for your area.
- **Website services:** Your biggest cost when it comes to running a digital product business is typically graphic design

services and subscriptions. This includes expenses such as monthly or yearly subscription fees for graphic design software and online platforms that you use to create and upload your designs. For example, I claim my subscriptions to Creative Fabrica and Canva Pro under web services. In addition, you can claim the cost for websites you use for Etsy keyword research (I use EtsyCheck and eRank) as well as costs from sites such as GoDaddy for any URL addresses and any website hosting (if you have a standalone website).

- **Advertising and marketing expenses:** Etsy will automatically deduct any charges for their ads, whether they are regular ads or off-site ads. However, if you advertise on Facebook or other social media websites, you will need to track those expenses yourself. You can see your yearly Facebook ad expenses in your Facebook account. If you order extra products for giveaways or collaborations, you should be able to claim those costs under marketing.

- **Home office expenses:** If you run your Etsy business from home, you may be able to claim a portion of your rent, utilities, and other home office expenses as a tax deduction.

- **Communications:** You can claim your internet service for your Etsy business. And if you use your smartphone for any business-related tasks, such as using design apps or tracking your shop through the Etsy app, you can claim that as well.

- **Business-related travel expenses:** If you attend trade shows or other events related to your business, you can claim the cost of transportation, lodging, and meals as a deduction.
- **Legal and professional fees:** This includes the cost of any legal or professional services you use in connection with your Etsy shop, such as accounting or tax preparation services.

Tracking your Etsy business expenses: There are several ways you can track your Etsy expenses to help manage your business and prepare for tax time. Here are a few options you can consider:

- **Use Etsy's built-in invoicing and payment tools to track your income and expenses.** These tools can help you keep track of the money you have earned, the fees you have paid to Etsy, and the expenses you have incurred in running your business.
- **Use accounting software to manage your finances.** There are many different accounting software options available, and some are specifically designed for small businesses or online marketplaces like Etsy. These tools track your income and expenses, generate reports, and prepare for tax time. TurboTax is the most popular of these services.
- **Keep detailed records of your income and expenses, such as receipts, invoices, and bank statements on a computer spreadsheet or even in a notebook.** Most of your income

and expenses will be recorded online on Etsy, your credit card statements, your bank statements, and the print provider you use. This makes transferring that data to your computer or paper easy.

- **Hire a certified public accountant or professional tax preparer**. Turning to an expert to handle your financial management and tax preparation can be money well spent. In addition to filing your taxes, they can also provide expert guidance on managing your finances.

My Way: Etsy automatically deducts fees and advertising costs from my account and only pays me the remaining balance, which is displayed under **Net Profit** in my Etsy account. At the end of the year, Etsy provides me with a 1099 form that lists my net profit after all of their fees have been deducted. On my end, I only need to keep track of my deductions that occur outside of the platform, meaning I do not need to track my Etsy fees or Etsy advertising expenses.

Remember that your gross sales are your sales BEFORE any fees or expenses are taken out. On Etsy, they will show you your NET profit after they take THEIR fees and advertising costs. However, as noted earlier, there are many more expenses you can claim as deductions when it comes time to file your taxes.

I use a basic spreadsheet to track my monthly expenses. Every month I record what I paid for web services (Creative Fabrica, Canva Pro, EtsyCheck, eRank, GoDaddy, etc.), advertising costs (Facebook ads or other advertising services), and communications expenses (internet and cell phone). Those are my only month-to-month business expenses. My accountant figures out how much I can claim for my home office, and since I don't do any driving for my digital product business, I can't claim mileage. I also don't travel for my Etsy business, so there are no hotels or plane tickets to claim. That means my only expense left is the fee my accountant charges to file my taxes.

At the end of the year, I tally every category of expenses to get the year-end total for each. For example, I will add up my internet and cell phone charges for each month and enter that number into my year-end communications field. Even though I have a CPA who files my taxes for me, I still provide him with these expense breakdowns so he can accurately file my returns.

At the end of January, I download my 1099 form from Etsy. I take that along with my list of year-end expenses to my accountant so he can file my taxes. Easy!

Disclaimer: Every state and country is different when it comes to taxes, so be sure to consult with a tax professional in your area for advice on how to manage your own Etsy bookkeeping.

CHAPTER TEN: HOW TO GROW YOUR DIGITAL PRODUCT BUSINESS

There is no doubt that Etsy is the best place to start a digital product business. The platform is perfectly designed to sell printables, and since Etsy is one of the largest online shopping websites, they have the traffic and customer base needed to successfully sell printables.

But while Etsy is the number one platform for a digital business, it isn't the only place where you can sell printable products. This chapter will focus on exploring these other platforms. Note that you don't have to sell even sell your digital products on Etsy; you can build an entire business on any of these websites. Just note that it can take more time to build a brand on these other platforms as none have the large built-in customer base that Etsy does.

Many sellers who sell digital downloads on sites other than or in addition to Etsy list their items on multiple websites to reach the most customers. However, it takes a lot more time and effort to list products on multiple sites. All have pros and cons; at the end of the day, only you can decide whether one, some, or all of these sites would work for your business.

Your Own Website: Developing a website where you can sell your own digital products can be a great way to establish your brand, expand your reach, and increase your revenue. Sites such as GoDaddy, Wix, and Shopify offer all of the tools you need to start selling your products directly to customers.

The pros of developing your own website include:

1. **More control:** When you sell digital products on your own website, you have complete control over the branding, design, and user experience.

2. **Less competition:** Unlike Etsy, where your competitor's products are shown right next to yours, on your own website, your products are the only ones customers see.

3. **Better data tracking:** With your own website, you can track visitor behavior, sales, and other metrics using analytics tools. This data can help you optimize your website and marketing efforts to improve conversions and revenue.

4. **Direct relationship with customers:** Selling on your own website allows you to build a direct relationship with your customers. You can communicate with them through email marketing, social media, and other channels to build brand loyalty.

5. **Better margins:** Without marketplace fees, you can potentially earn higher margins on your digital products. You can also set your pricing and discounts without having to be in direct competition with other sellers.

6. **More revenue opportunities:** Programs such as Google AdSense and Amazon Associates allow you to earn more money by placing ads on your website.

The cons of creating your own website include:

1. **More work:** Creating and maintaining your own website requires more effort and resources than selling on a marketplace like Etsy. You will need to manage website design, hosting, security, and payment processing, which is not only time-consuming but also more expensive. And because digital products require the transfer of a file versus the shipping of a physical product, you will have to manually email customers their orders.

2. **Marketing is your responsibility:** When you sell on a platform such as Etsy, you benefit from their marketing and promotion efforts, which bring millions of customers to their site. When you sell on your own website, you are responsible for driving traffic and promoting your products through social media, email marketing, and other channels. You may need to invest in advertising on Facebook and Google to draw in shoppers, which will cost significantly more than the fees you pay on Etsy for them to handle marketing.

3. **No built-in audience:** Marketplaces like Etsy have a built-in audience of buyers looking for unique items, including

digital and printable products. With your own website, you will need to build your own audience and attract customers through SEO, advertising, and other tactics. This will take considerable time and money to achieve.

4. **Technical expertise required:** Building and managing your own website requires some technical knowledge, especially if you want to customize your website and add advanced features. You may need to hire a web developer or learn some coding skills. To sell digital files, you will need to find a system where customers automatically have access to the items they buy or you will have to manually email all files you sell.

5. **Payments and taxes:** Not only will you need to implement a payment system to collect money and pay yourself, but you will also be responsible for charging and remitting sales tax to the American states that require it. The tax implications of selling on your own website when it comes to collecting sales tax is the main reason many sellers decide not to develop their own websites as it's much easier to let sites like Etsy do it.

Creative Market: Creative Market is a platform where designers, developers, and other creators can sell and buy digital assets such as fonts, graphics, templates, themes, and more. The platform was founded in 2012 and has since grown into a popular marketplace for digital products, making it a popular choice for Etsy sellers to expand their businesses.

Creative Market boasts over 3 million members and more than 7 million products sold. The company is headquartered in San Francisco, California, and has a small team of employees who work remotely around the world. In addition to its core marketplace for buying and selling digital assets, Creative Market also offers various resources and tools to help creators succeed. These include blog posts, tutorials, and design assets to help creators improve their skills and produce higher-quality work.

Creative Market handles payment processing for sellers through their own platform, which allows them to receive payments directly from buyers. When a buyer purchases a product from a seller on Creative Market, the payment is processed through Creative Market's payment system and then transferred to the seller's account on the platform.

Creative Market charges a fee of 30% on each sale made by a seller on their platform. This means that if a seller sells a product for $10, Creative Market will keep $3 and the seller will receive $7.

As for sales tax, Creative Market collects and remits sales tax on behalf of sellers for transactions that occur in the United States. This means that if a seller makes a sale to a buyer in the US, Creative Market will calculate and collect the appropriate sales tax, and then remit it to the appropriate tax authority. Sellers are not responsible for collecting or remitting sales tax on their own for transactions made on the Creative Market platform.

Creative Market's platform is designed to make it easy for creators to sell their digital products and for buyers to find high-quality and unique assets. The platform offers a range of digital products across various categories, including fonts, graphics, templates, themes, photos, and more. Sellers can create their own shops on the platform to showcase their products and set their own prices.

The top digital products that sellers offer on Creative Market are:

1. **Fonts:** Fonts are a popular category on Creative Market, as designers and creators are always looking for new and unique typefaces to use in their projects. Handwritten fonts, serif, sans-serif fonts, and display fonts are all in high demand.

2. **Graphics:** Graphics such as icons, illustrations, and patterns are also popular on Creative Market. These can be used in a variety of design projects, from website design to social media graphics.

3. **Templates:** Templates for resumes, social media posts, and presentations are in high demand, as they provide a quick and easy way for people to create professional-looking designs without starting from scratch.

4. **Themes:** Website and e-commerce themes are a popular category on Creative Market, as they provide a customizable and cost-effective solution for creating a professional-looking website or online store.

5. **Add-ons:** Add-ons such as Photoshop brushes, Lightroom presets, and Procreate brushes are also popular on the platform. These can help designers and creators streamline their workflows and create more unique and professional-looking designs.

6. **Photos:** High-quality stock photos are always in demand on Creative Market, as they can be used in a variety of design projects, from website backgrounds to social media graphics.

7. **3D models:** 3D models and assets are also becoming more popular on the platform, as more designers and creators are exploring 3D design and animation.

Gumroad: Gumroad is arguably the most popular platform for selling digital products outside of Etsy. Gumroad was founded in 2011 by Sahil Lavingia, a former early employee of Pinterest. The company's mission is to help creators monetize their work and share it with the world, making it easier for them to sell digital products such as eBooks, music, videos, software, and more.

Since its founding, Gumroad has grown into a popular platform for creators, with over 50,000 creators and more than $400 million in sales processed. The company is headquartered in San Francisco, California, and has a small team of employees who work remotely around the world.

Gumroad also handles payment processing for sellers through its platform. When a buyer purchases a product from a seller on Gumroad, the payment is processed through Gumroad's payment system and then transferred to the seller's account on the platform.

Gumroad charges a fee of 8.5% + 30 cents per transaction for sellers on their platform. This means that if a seller sells a product for $10, Gumroad will keep $1.15 and the seller will receive $8.55.

Gumroad provides sellers with the option to pass on sales tax to buyers or to absorb the cost themselves. If a seller chooses to pass on sales tax to buyers, Gumroad will automatically calculate and add the appropriate sales tax to the purchase price of the product based on the buyer's location. However, sellers are responsible for remitting the sales tax to the appropriate tax authority on their own. If a seller chooses to absorb the cost of sales tax, Gumroad will not add sales tax to the purchase price, and the seller will be responsible for paying any sales tax owed to the appropriate tax authority.

In addition to its core platform for selling digital products, Gumroad also offers a range of tools and resources to help creators grow their businesses, including email marketing tools, analytics, and integrations with other platforms like WordPress and Mailchimp.

The top digital products that sellers offer on Gumroad are:

1. **eBooks and digital guides:** eBooks and digital guides are a popular category on Gumroad, particularly in areas like self-help, business, and personal finance. These can be sold as PDFs, EPUBs, or other file formats.

2. **Online courses and tutorials:** Online courses and tutorials are also a popular category on Gumroad. These can include video courses, webinars, and other types of educational content.

3. **Music and audio files:** Music tracks, sound effects, and audio files are also popular on Gumroad. These can be sold as individual tracks or as part of a larger collection.

4. **Digital art and design assets:** Digital art and design assets such as Photoshop brushes, vectors, and textures are also in demand on Gumroad. These can help designers and artists create more unique and professional-looking designs.

5. **Software and digital tools:** Software and digital tools such as plugins, scripts, and templates are also popular on the platform. These can help creators streamline their workflows and create more complex and advanced projects.

6. **Photography and stock photos:** High-quality stock photos and photography assets are also in demand on Gumroad, as

they can be used in a variety of design projects, from website backgrounds to social media graphics.

7. **3D models and assets:** 3D models and assets are becoming more popular on the platform, as more designers and creators are exploring 3D design and animation.

WooCommerce: WooCommerce is a free and open-source e-commerce platform for WordPress. It was created in 2011 by Mike Jolley and James Koster and was later acquired by Automattic, the company behind WordPress.com. However, unlike other platforms that provide a range of backend services, WooCommerce does not.

For example, WooCommerce does not handle payment processing on its own. Instead, payment processing is handled through payment gateway plugins that can be integrated into WooCommerce. WooCommerce supports a wide range of payment gateways, including PayPal, Stripe, Square, and many others. When a buyer purchases a product from a seller on WooCommerce, the payment is processed through the payment gateway that the seller has integrated into their WooCommerce store.

As for fees, WooCommerce itself does not charge any transaction fees to sellers. However, the payment gateway that a seller uses may charge transaction fees. For example, Stripe charges a fee of 2.9% + 30 cents per transaction for US-based sellers.

WooCommerce does not automatically collect and remit sales tax on behalf of sellers. Instead, sellers are responsible for setting up and configuring sales tax collection and remittance through a plugin or manually. WooCommerce provides various sales tax plugins that can be integrated with the platform, including WooCommerce Tax and TaxJar. These plugins can automatically calculate the appropriate sales tax based on the buyer's location and collect it on behalf of the seller. However, sellers are still responsible for remitting the sales tax to the appropriate tax authority.

Digital businesses that sell on WooCommerce typically have a strong technical understanding or access to technical expertise to set up and manage their e-commerce store. They may also have existing relationships with payment gateway providers or accounting and tax experts who can help them navigate the complexities of payment processing and sales tax collection.

The top digital products that sellers offer on WooCommerce are:

1. **Software and digital tools:** WooCommerce can be used to sell digital tools and software such as plugins, scripts, and templates.
2. **Online courses and tutorials:** WooCommerce can also be used to sell online courses and tutorials, which can be delivered as video, audio, or text-based content. These can

include courses on topics such as business, marketing, and personal development.

3. **Music and audio files:** WooCommerce can be used to sell music tracks, sound effects, and audio files. These can be sold as individual tracks or as part of a larger collection.

4. **eBooks and digital guides:** WooCommerce is a popular platform for selling eBooks and digital guides, particularly in areas such as self-help, business, and personal finance.

5. **Digital art and design assets:** WooCommerce can be used to sell digital art and design assets such as Photoshop brushes, vectors, and textures.

6. **Photography and stock photos:** WooCommerce can be used to sell high-quality stock photos and photography assets, which can be used in a variety of design projects.

7. **3D models and assets:** WooCommerce can also be used to sell 3D models and assets, which are becoming more popular as more designers and creators explore 3D design and animation

Creative Fabrica: While many sellers use Creative Fabrica for elements used to create digital products if you are a designer and have created your own original products from scratch, you can sell your items there, too. Here's how:

1. Sellers can create a shop on Creative Fabrica to showcase and sell their digital products. To get started, they need to

sign up for a seller account and apply, which includes a review of their portfolio and product quality.

2. Once approved, sellers can upload their digital products to their shop and set their own prices. Creative Fabrica takes a commission on each sale, which covers payment processing and platform fees.

3. Buyers can browse Creative Fabrica to find digital products that fit their needs. They can purchase products directly from the seller's shop using a variety of payment methods, including credit cards and PayPal.

4. Creative Fabrica offers a range of digital products across various categories, including fonts, graphics, templates, themes, and more. Sellers can also offer free products to attract potential customers and build their brand.

5. Creative Fabrica provides tools and resources to help sellers optimize their product listings and reach a wider audience. Sellers can use analytics to track sales and visitor behavior, and they can participate in promotional events and sales to increase visibility and sales.

Creative Fabrica handles payment processing and tax collection for sellers on their platform. When a buyer purchases a product from a seller on Creative Fabrica, the payment is processed through Creative Fabrica's payment system and then transferred to the seller's account on the platform.

Creative Fabrica charges a fee of 40% on each sale made by a seller on their platform. This means that if a seller sells a product for $10, Creative Fabrica will keep $4 and the seller will receive $6.

As for sales tax, Creative Fabrica collects and remits sales tax on behalf of sellers for transactions that occur in the European Union (EU). This means that if a seller makes a sale to a buyer in the EU, Creative Fabrica will calculate and collect the appropriate sales tax, and then remit it to the appropriate tax authority. Sellers are not responsible for collecting or remitting sales tax on their own for transactions made on the Creative Fabrica platform.

For sales outside the EU, sellers are responsible for complying with any applicable tax laws and regulations. Sellers must set their prices that include any applicable taxes, and Creative Fabrica will not collect or remit taxes on their behalf for sales made outside the EU.

Creative Fabrica offers two ways for sellers to make money on the platform: selling elements individually and through the subscription model.

Selling elements individually: Sellers can upload their digital products to Creative Fabrica and sell them individually. They can set their own prices for each product, and Creative Fabrica takes a commission on each sale. This model is similar to other digital marketplaces, and sellers earn money for each sale of their products.

Subscription model: Creative Fabrica also offers a subscription model for customers, which gives them access to a large library of digital products. Sellers can participate in this model by uploading their products to the subscription library. They earn a portion of the subscription revenue based on how many times their products are downloaded by subscribers. The more popular their products are, the more money they can earn through the subscription model.

Overextending Yourself: Etsy, your own website, Creative Market, Gumroad, WooCommerce, Creative Fabrica. Thinking about building your business across all of these platforms can be both exciting and overwhelming. On the one hand, having your products for sale on multiple websites gives you more opportunities to make sales. On the other hand, it takes a lot of time and effort to create and list digital products for sale on just Etsy, let alone these other sites.

Do you need to list your digital products on more than one website? Absolutely not. This is your business, and you need to figure out what works best for you. Most sellers start with Etsy, prefer Etsy, and only sell on Etsy. Other sellers, for whatever reason, don't like Etsy at all and skip it altogether. And some sellers start on Etsy and slowly grow their business on other websites.

Just remember that overextending yourself can result in lower product quality and customer service issues. Only after you have mastered one website and have built it to a successful level should you consider expanding to other websites. If you find that selling digital products on Etsy alone is all you can handle, that's okay, too!

CONCLUSION

Selling digital products on Etsy is a great business opportunity for people of all skill levels. Whether you are a designer who plans to create products from scratch or are a novice who will utilize graphic subscription services to create your items, selling digital downloads is something almost anyone can do.

Etsy offers a user-friendly platform that is specifically designed for creators to sell all sorts of digital products. With Etsy's built-in features, anyone can easily start their own digital shop selling to customers around the world. And with Etsy's payment processing and tax collection handled for sellers, you as a business owner can focus your energy on creating and listing products.

While there are other platforms available for selling digital products, Etsy has the advantage. It has a large and active community of buyers looking for unique and high-quality digital products, and it offers a range of tools and resources to help sellers succeed. Additionally, Etsy's commission fees are relatively low compared to other platforms, making it the best place to start earning money.

However, like any business venture, selling digital products on Etsy requires hard work, dedication, and persistence. You need to create high-quality, unique, and valuable products that stand out in a crowded market, and you need to market and promote your products effectively to reach your target audience. You also need to stay on top of industry trends, update your products regularly, and provide excellent customer service to build a loyal customer base.

That being said, if you're willing to put in the effort and take a strategic approach, selling digital products on Etsy is a fantastic home-based business. I hope this guide has provided you with the knowledge, tools, and inspiration to start and grow your digital product business on Etsy and perhaps beyond.

Good luck and happy selling!

ABOUT THE AUTHOR

Ann Eckhart is a writer, entrepreneur, and online content creator based in Iowa. She has authored numerous books about home-based e-commerce businesses on topics including reselling, self-publishing, print-on-demand, and social media. You can find all her titles at www.AnnEckhart.com.

You can follow Ann Eckhart on the following social media platforms:

Facebook @anneckhart

Instagram @ann_marie_eckhart

YouTube @anneckhart

Printed in Great Britain
by Amazon

31533128R00139